The Multicultural
Math Classroom

The Multicultural Math Classroom

Bringing in the World

Claudia Zaslavsky

HEINEMANN
Portsmouth, NH

Heinemann
A division of Reed Elsevier Inc.
361 Hanover Street
Portsmouth, NH 03801-3912

Offices and agents throughout the world

Library of Congress Cataloging-in-Publication Data
Zaslavsky, Claudia.
    The multicultural math classroom : bringing in the world / Claudia Zaslavsky.
        p.   cm.
    Includes bibliographical references and index.
    ISBN 0-435-08373-2
    1. Mathematics—Study and teaching (Elementary)   2. Multicultural education.   I. Title.
QA135.5.Z367   1996
372.7—dc20   95-35677
                                                                  CIP

Editor: Toby Gordon
Production: Vicki Kasabian
Text design: Joni Doherty
Cover design: Studio Nine
Cover photograph: Vicki Kasabian

Printed in the United States of America on acid-free paper
07   VP   10

Contents

Acknowledgments

My interest in equity issues in mathematics education began when I started to teach secondary-level mathematics in a New York State district that had been integrated by busing in 1951. My involvement in multicultural perspectives in the mathematics curriculum developed as I was doing research for my book *Africa Counts: Number and Pattern in African Culture*, originally published in 1973. For many years thereafter I was virtually a voice crying in the wilderness. The climate has changed in the last few years. Now I am a welcome speaker at mathematics education conferences, and publishers seek my services. Multicultural mathematics education has joined the mainstream.

I wish to thank the educators who sent me descriptions of their lessons or allowed me to observe their classes in action: Gwendolyn Clinkscales, Grace Cohen, Beverly J. Ferrucci, Barbara Brown Gathers, Esther Ilutsik, Kathryn Schubeck, Lawrence Shirley, and Marilyn Strutchens. Beatrice Lumpkin generously shared the letters she received from Barbara Gathers' students in response to her books on ancient Egypt. Principal Mark Kavarsky, teachers, and students at Salomé Ureña Middle Academies were very helpful, particularly librarian Judith Schaffner and the students whose work and photographs I include in this book. Teachers Iris Mitchell and I. Knesz at PS189M kindly granted permission to include photographs of their students' creations. I am grateful to Jerry Lipka and Claudette Bradley, directors of the Yup'ik math and science project in Alaska, and to the participants in the meetings for an enlightening experience, much information, and interesting photographs.

A special thanks to my husband, Sam Zaslavsky, for his many photographs and his involvement in all stages of this book.

Preface

There is a growing body of literature on multicultural education, stimulated by concerns for equity, equality, and excellence. Educators know that in the world of the future all citizens must have the knowledge and skill to solve the problems of an increasingly complex society. Teachers realize that students are most motivated when they are actively involved in their own learning while dealing with the issues of greatest concern to themselves and their communities. Curriculum developers recognize the need to bring multicultural perspectives into such subject areas as social studies, language arts, music, and fine arts, to introduce students to the contributions that all peoples have made in these fields and to the stories they have to tell.

For several reasons, the literature on multicultural perspectives in mathematics education is relatively sparse. This is beginning to change as the National Council of Teachers of Mathematics, as well as educators in the field, recognizes the need to be concerned about equity, equality, and excellence. No longer can we be satisfied with cultivating a white-male mathematical elite while the rest of the population lags behind. No longer can we ignore the mathematical heritage of a major segment of the student population: females and people of color. All peoples engage in mathematical activities to the extent of their needs and interests; how they carry out these activities varies from one culture to another. By introducing multicultural perspectives into the mathematics curriculum we can engage students' imagination and help them develop skills in critical thinking and analysis that can be applied to all areas of life.

In this book I lay out a rationale for multicultural mathematics education. I quote and refer to writings of both authorities in general multicultural education and those who are concerned with equity issues in mathematics. I describe the work of mathematics educators who are bringing multicultural perspectives into their classrooms and teacher education programs.

The main body of this book—Chapters 4–11—discusses multicultural mathematics curriculum. Each of these chapters begins with a listing of the mathematical topics, the cultural connections, and links to other subject areas. Since every lesson involves language arts and social studies, those connections are not cited in the introductions but are evident in the activities suggested in the chapters. Students should learn the locations of the societies under discussion and be able to find them on a map. Many of the lessons also involve dramatic role play and other forms of artistic expression. I also furnish background information about each topic's history and development, as well as references for both teachers and students.

In accordance with the *Curriculum and Evaluation Standards for School Mathematics* (National Council of Teachers of Mathematics 1989), I emphasize the problem-solving process and the connections to the development of skills in reasoning and communication, as well as the more specific mathematical skills, including the use of manipulatives and technology. Most of the lessons suggest some form of writing or artistic work on paper; these items can then be collected into portfolios that can form the basis for assessment.

The suggested activities encourage cooperation, creativity, and critical thinking, and their variety should appeal to a diversity of learning styles and backgrounds. Because the activities are open-ended, they are able to engage students of varied interests and ability levels. I do not give specific grade levels for each activity; I know from experience that teachers are creative in adapting curriculum ideas to their own grade levels.

Education in general and mathematics education in particular are undergoing great changes. We are in the midst of movements to restructure the schools and to make teachers and students responsible for their own teaching and learning. Mathematics educators are urging curriculum revisions that integrate mathematics with other subject areas and that emphasize cooperative learning and student involvement in long-range projects in addition to or instead of the drill and practice of isolated skills. Test developers are beginning to take these trends into consideration as they design instruments that will truly assess the new kind of learning. Parents and the community are invited to participate in the work of the schools. All these conditions are favorable to the adoption of multicultural perspectives in mathematics education.

The final chapter of this book deals with some of the problems teachers may encounter in their attempts to put multicultural mathematics education into practice. There is also an extensive list of resources for further exploration by both teachers and students.

Chapter 1

Overview of Multicultural Mathematics Education

Three Common Questions

"What do you mean by *multicultural* mathematics? Isn't math the same all over the world?"

This question often comes from high school and college mathematics instructors, who are accustomed to formal presentations of abstract, contextless mathematics. It's true that people all over the world engage in mathematical activities to the extent of their needs and interests. They all count objects, they measure various quantities, they invent calendars and other ways to describe the passage of time, they design works of art, they plan buildings, and they play games that involve mathematical concepts. Furthermore, they invent terminology that enables them to discuss these activities. But each culture, each group, solves these problems in its own way. Very often new ideas are borrowed from other cultures, just as the numerals with which we calculate so efficiently originated in India and entered Europe through transmission by Arabic-speaking North Africans. Much of the foundation for the math that our children learn in elementary and middle school was laid in Africa and Asia.

In some societies these ideas are written down in books labeled *mathematics*. In other societies mathematical concepts are incorporated into everyday activities but are not specifically called *mathematics*, nor do these societies call the practitioners *mathematicians*. Students of any age can be informal mathematicians. We can challenge them to apply mathematical ideas to problems that confronted people in the past and that we encounter in our contemporary culture.

1

"We have some African American students in our school. I suppose we should have your book *Africa Counts***?"**
Multicultural mathematics education is for all people, whatever their ethnic/racial heritage, their gender, or their socioeconomic status. By bringing multicultural perspectives into the math curriculum, teachers can enrich students' learning, giving them a broad view of the scope of mathematics and its place in the development of societies. According to the *Curriculum and Evaluation Standards for School Mathematics* (NCTM 1989), "Students should have numerous and varied experiences related to the cultural, historical, and scientific evolution of mathematics so that they can appreciate the role of mathematics in the development of our contemporary society and explore relationships among mathematics and the disciplines it serves: the physical and life sciences, the social sciences, and the humanities" (5).

"I asked my math teacher about African math, and she said there is none. Is she right?"
People look for affirmation of their cultural heritage. Each individual wants to know, Where do I fit in? This question doesn't contradict the statement that multicultural math is for everyone. In each class and with each group, the teacher can tailor the curriculum to emphasize those aspects that are of the greatest interest to that specific community. Students can take pride in the contributions of their people, and at the same time learn to appreciate what others have accomplished. Self-esteem is a necessary component of learning.

Our Multicultural Nation

In her book *Planning and Organizing for Multicultural Instruction* (1994), Gwendolyn Baker writes:

> Our nation's culturally diverse and pluralistic nature makes it imperative for schools to provide educational experiences and training that will not only prepare students to live successfully in a diverse nation but also to base educational content and process on the cultural histories, experiences, languages, and lifestyles of all students. The failure of the public schools to

> provide this type of instruction lies in the history of American
> public education. (5)

Few countries of the world have the tremendous diversity of population that we enjoy in the United States. Most of the people living in our country today can trace their roots to other continents. Some came willingly, others were forced to leave their homelands, and in the process the indigenous population of this continent was virtually wiped out. Not all groups have participated equally in the leadership of the country. During most of the past centuries the leaders of government, economic life, and academic institutions have been white men of western European heritage. It is only in the past few decades, as a result of long struggles, that women and people of color have begun to take their rightful places in the life of our country.

We still have a long way to go before we can say that all people have equal opportunity to become productive and respected citizens. Recent immigrants are resented by those whose ancestors arrived some time ago. The current population of Native Americans is far smaller than the number at the time Europeans first invaded the Americas. People of African heritage have yet to overcome the effects of the racism that was used to justify the slavery of their ancestors. People of color are disproportionately represented among those living in poverty, the unemployed, and school dropouts. Women of all backgrounds are far from the attainment of equality with white men in status and income.

What Is Multiculturalism in Education?

Multiculturalism in education has been interpreted in many ways. It may mean introducing some ethnic/racial content into the curriculum. In mathematics textbooks this may take the form of one page in each chapter devoted to a description of a mathematical practice of the ancient Chinese or a brief mention of Benjamin Banneker, the eighteenth-century African American self-taught mathematician, astronomer, and surveyor, a page that a teacher may very well skip under pressure to drill her students for the upcoming achievement tests. Some publishers put out ancillary materials of this nature that can be used either in association with specific chapters in their textbooks or independently.

In this context, *multicultural* means *multiethnic*. It refers to people of backgrounds that are broadly classified as African American, European American, Latino/Latina or Hispanic American, Native American, and Asian American, and to subdivisions of these broad groups—Italian, Jewish, Jamaican, Mexican, Chinese, Cherokee, to name just a few. These categories are often determined by law or by social custom rather than by geography or genetics. For example, many states had laws, only recently abolished, to the effect that anyone with at least one-eighth African ancestry was "Negro." On the other hand, children of Dominican heritage in a local middle school deny that they have any African ancestry, although their skins are as dark as that of the African American teacher who told me about this. They prefer to be considered "Latino."

The inclusion of this type of material marks a good beginning on the part of publishers and indicates a recognition of the need for at least a certain type of multicultural infusion, but it is only a beginning. University of Wisconsin professor Walter Secada, in his article "Towards a Consciously Multicultural Mathematics Curriculum" (1994), goes so far as to suggest that these efforts on the part of publishers might, in fact, convey the wrong messages. He describes "three major threats: (a) superficial treatment of mathematical content, (b) irrelevance of content and contexts to the lives of diverse students, and (c) the possibility of re-creating stereotypes, but in different ways" (240).

I interpret *multicultural* to mean more than *multiethnic*. The term *cultural group* may refer to women and men, to geographic regions, to people in specific occupations or age groups. Local communities also have their own cultures and their own issues. What is needed is a revision of the whole curriculum, all subject areas, to include those groups—women, working people, ethnic/racial groups—whose contributions and place in history have been distorted, marginalized, or ignored completely. I include the issues and problems that the students and their communities face today.

Often the term *minority* is applied to certain ethnic/racial groups. This word may carry the implication of a lower status than the "white" majority. Furthermore, the word *minorities* lumps together many diverse groups as though they are all the same. From the point of view of numbers, the so-called minorities will soon constitute about half of the population of our schools, and in many large cities they are already the majority. There is not a good overall term for those whom government reports and the media designate as "minorities." I use the expression *people of color*, a more acceptable term than some others.

Goals of Multicultural Education

In their farsighted *Teaching with a Multicultural Perspective* (1994), Leonard and Patricia T. Davidman synthesize the concepts of such leaders in the field as James Banks, Carl Grant, Christine Sleeter, H. Prentice Baptiste, Jr., and Mira Baptiste. They list the following goals as a "useful point of departure for K–8 educators seeking to learn more ways to create multicultural education in their respective grades" (2):

> (1) educational equity; (2) empowerment of students and their parents; (3) cultural pluralism in society; (4) intercultural/ interethnic/intergroup understanding and harmony in the classroom, school, and community; (5) an expanded knowledge of various cultural and ethnic groups; (6) the development of students, parents, and practitioners (teachers, nurses, counselors, principals, curriculum coordinators, etc.) whose thoughts and actions are guided by an informed and inquisitive multicultural perspective. (2)

Let's look at how these goals apply to mathematics education.

Educational equity

The goal of educational equity is of the utmost importance if we are to achieve multiculturalism. The influential *Curriculum and Evaluation Standards* (NCTM 1989) emphasizes that "it is crucial that conscious efforts be made to encourage all students, especially young women and minorities, to pursue mathematics" (68). Our educational system has been a reflection of our society. We have produced a well-trained scientific elite comprising mainly white middle- and upper-class males, while the rest of the population has been left behind.

Our schools today are not equitable. Wealthy districts spend as much as five times per student more than do poor districts in the same state. When we note that in 1990 one in five children in the United States under the age of eighteen lived in poverty but that almost half of black children and two out of five Latino children lived below the government's poverty line, we see that children of color are even more likely than white children to be shortchanged. Schools in low-income areas are likely to have few computers, outdated textbooks, inadequate science laboratories, and overcrowded buildings in a state of disrepair. Their low-paid teachers may have had inadequate training and experience. In many states the courts have ruled that funding must be equalized, yet little has been done to carry out these mandates. Meanwhile millions of young people are denied equal educational opportunity.

Equalizing funding for all school districts will only begin to solve the problem of school finance in poor districts. Additional resources are needed to replace deteriorated facilities, to upgrade teacher education, to deal with the influx of students who do not speak English, and to handle the many problems that low-income children must face.

We must also be concerned with equal treatment and equal educational outcomes for all students regardless of their ethnicity and race, their gender, and their socioeconomic background. One barrier to this aspect of educational equity is the practice of placing students into different tracks—remedial, average, enriched, and gifted. Once students are placed in a low track, often in kindergarten or first grade, they are unlikely ever to advance to a higher level. On the contrary, they usually fall further behind and may drop out before completing secondary school. The basis for sorting students is often a score on a standardized test. A student with a low reading score may be a math genius but is placed, nevertheless, in a remedial class for all subjects. In their 1987 study *The Underachieving Curriculum*, Curtis C. McKnight and his colleagues examined the eighth-grade math curriculum in various schools in the United States. They found four levels, ranging from algebra to remedial. Ironically, when they investigated the math test scores of students entering these programs, they found a large overlap; in fact, the lowest scores in the algebra strand were below three quarters of the scores in the remedial classes. The most drastic impact of these inequities falls on ''minority'' and low-income young people. Once they are in the lowest track, with its ''dumbed down'' curriculum, they are virtually deprived of the opportunity to take algebra and other academic math courses.

On a more personal note, my granddaughter is an eighth grader in an alternative K–8 school, where half the students are children of color and the other half are white. Her math teacher told parents that he had formerly placed only recommended students in algebra. Algebra is considered the gateway to all higher-level courses. Recently he was persuaded by an elementary school teacher to offer algebra to every eighth-grade student. Subsequently he couldn't tell the difference between those who were recommended and those who weren't!

As I write, a debate is raging over the recently published *The Bell Curve* (1994), by Charles Murray and Richard J. Herrnstein, in which the authors revive the old stereotype that blacks are inferior to whites in innate cognitive ability. Furthermore, they claim that intervention strategies are of no avail in improving the performance of low-achieving groups. Their arguments are based chiefly on I.Q. and other standardized tests, tests that have been exposed as biased and having little to do with the capacity to learn. In my own *Fear of Math: How to Get Over It and Get On with Your Life* (1994), I devote an entire chapter ("Myths of Innate Inferiority") to exposing the belief that certain large categories of people—women, African Americans, Latinos/as, and working-class people, for example—are incapable of learning high-level mathematics. As I discovered in the course of my research, even teachers are guilty, perhaps unconsciously, of this type of stereotyping. Unfortunately, racism, classism, and sexism are alive and well in our society.

Empowerment
I believe that empowerment is the most important goal of education. Empowerment of students in mathematics means that they have acquired the necessary skills to function in our technological society. It implies that they are learning to work independently and with other people to solve problems requiring mathematical knowledge. It means that students are able to direct their own learning, to approach new tasks with confidence in their ability to handle them. We know now that people must construct their own knowledge, that mere memorization of rote procedures does not empower students in mathematics. Material that is memorized without understanding is soon forgotten or applied incorrectly.

How can we encourage students to think mathematically, so that they can solve real-world problems? Certainly not by having them do page after page of arithmetic drill exercises. To solve real-world problems they must have practice solving real-world problems, the kinds of problems that people must deal with in their daily lives. Math should be presented in a meaningful context, whether relating to the students' own society or to the problems that confonted people in the past and/or in other parts of our world. In order to empower students we must offer them a mathematics curriculum that is multicultural and interdisciplinary. Empowerment means that students will be able to analyze the statistics and graphs they read in the media, to apply their mathematical knowledge to the problems of society, and to take appropriate action as citizens of their communities.

Many young African Americans, Latinos and Latinas, and girls of all backgrounds have internalized the stereotypes about their lack of math ability. This belief may discourage children in those groups from doing well in math. Unaware of the many women and people of African American or Hispanic background who have done well in math-related fields, they may believe that math is "for boys only" or "for white people only," and shun the subject. Introducing them to successful people who look like them may encourage these young people to persist in mathematics.

Teachers, too, must be empowered. One aspect of this empowerment is having confidence in their mathematical knowledge or acquiring the mathematical knowledge they for whatever reason lack. Another is being free to shape the content and style of their lessons to suit the students with whom they work so that every student has a successful experience in learning.

Parents and caretakers need to be empowered to become involved in their children's education, a factor that influences how well students learn. Many parents feel incapable of understanding the mathematics that their children are doing. (Family Math is one program that enables family members and children to work together and have fun while they cooperate in doing all kinds of math—see Resources, page 221.)

Cultural pluralism

This goal implies that students respect and appreciate individuals and groups that are different from themselves. Teachers can encourage girls and boys to learn to work together in cooperative learning groups. In some classrooms it may be possible to form groups that include children of different ethnic/racial backgrounds, a most effective way to overcome stereotypes about people who are different from oneself.

Intergroup/intragroup harmony
Multicultural perspectives help children counter stereotypes and lead to an appreciation of the mathematical ideas developed by all societies, including the cultural groups with which they identify. Research about the participation of women in mathematics reveals that men's attitudes are a key factor in discouraging females from continuing in math. Teachers must also be aware of their own prejudices concerning the ability of girls and students from certain ethnic/racial groups to learn mathematics.

Expanded multicultural/multiethnic knowledge
Students need to learn about the mathematical involvement of their own and other societies and groups. This knowledge should increase students' self-esteem and self-confidence. According to the NCTM (1989), "Students' cultural backgrounds should be integrated into the learning experience" (68). The section of this book dealing with curriculum expands upon this goal. I will give one example here.

Professor Lawrence Shirley is now a mathematics instructor at Towson State University, near Baltimore, having taught for many years at a university in northern Nigeria. He works with both teacher-preparation classes and a special enrichment class for children from urban middle schools. Larry sent me a description of the multicultural aspects of his curriculum and the reactions of two dissimilar groups of students. (For additional information about his work, see Lawrence Shirley, "Activities from African Calendar and Time Customs" [*Mathematics Teaching in the Middle School*, in press].)

About his teacher-preparation students he writes:

> The classes are about ninety percent white, but many are prospective teachers in schools which have high minority enrollments. Hence, as preparation, they seem eager to learn examples to help "multiculturalize" their classes and they take note of how they would use these examples themselves.
>
> I often teach the classes oware [see page 189] and let them

■ FIGURE 1–1 Oware game board on kente cloth. Collection of D. W. Crowe, Madison, Wisconsin

try to discern strategies from playing one or two games. . . . I usually have actual wooden boards to show how the game is played in West Africa, and the authenticity adds to the interest of the class. A surprising highlight of linking to home culture came last semester, when one of my students, a Filipina-American, suddenly noted that her grandmother in the Philippines played a similar game.

I also use some counting words in Nigerian languages to demonstrate variety in numeration systems. This is valuable in class since all European languages that the class is familiar with seem to have similar base ten structures. I show a brief grouping by five in Fulfulde (similar to Roman numerals, it jumps to groupings by ten and five); Yoruba (which uses groups of ten, but has twenty as its major grouping pattern, and also includes subtraction in its number names); and my special favorite, Mada, which groups in dozens. This has applications both in the History of Math course, comparing

with ancient counting patterns, and in elementary math
methodology, as enrichment for instruction in place value.

He goes on to describe the Saturday classes of middle-grade students,
about ninety percent of them African American. On the first day, after a
campus tour and lunch, they come back to the classroom:

> They are surprised to see the classroom transformed with
> Kente cloth from Ghana, tie-dye from Sierra Leone, oware
> boards, a map of Africa, and me now wearing a Hausa caftan
> costume and an embroidered cap. Is this math?
>
> Yes, it is a session labeled "African math" where they learn
> of mathematical work done in ancient African empires and the
> long distance traders along the coast near Mombasa and across
> the Sahara from Kano and Timbuktu.
>
> To begin, they have to figure out the day of the week they
> were born on in order to learn their "day-name" from Akan
> [Ghana] or Hausa [northern Nigeria] culture. This isn't a
> mathematical activity in Africa since children are named
> directly for the day of the week of their birth, but since most
> Americans don't know this information, it becomes a problem-
> solving activity for middle school children. They are especially
> motivated since this age is always a time for playing with
> alternative names and especially since several of the Akan
> names have become well known as "African names." Baltimore
> has a Congressman named Kweisi, derived from the Akan
> Sunday boy name of Kwasi, and a popular television show has
> a character with the Saturday boy name of Kwame. (I also
> point out that it was the name of the man who led Ghana to
> independence, though I notice that few have heard of Kwame
> Nkrumah.) They busy themselves counting how their birthday
> has moved through the week and then proudly wear name
> tags with their day names.
>
> They, like the university students, also enjoy learning about
> Nigerian counting words and playing oware. They make more
> effort than the university students at trying to pronounce the
> counting words and seem just about as fast at recognizing
> patterns. I'm pleased to see that a few have played oware.

They take it upon themselves to be the experts who help the others learn how the game is played. I usually see a few in hot competition and they start thinking of strategies even as they play. I hope and believe (but don't have a good way to check) that they later teach the game to their friends and siblings at home.

Larry's examples show that although all societies count, ethnic groups within Nigeria vary widely in the way they form their systems of number words, what they use as the base, or grouping, unit, and how they combine these units. On the other hand, peoples in widely separated parts of the world play different versions of the same game, indicating that societies borrowed from one another.

Larry implies that the prospect of teaching classes of "minority" children motivates his predominantly white university students to become interested in "multiculturalizing" the mathematics curriculum. He contrasts the enthusiasm displayed by the middle school students, most of them African American, in learning African number words, with that of the predominantly white university students. His report makes it clear that the children identified with their African heritage, and this affirmation boosted their self-esteem. The fact that Professor Shirley is white seemed not to dampen their enthusiasm.

The development of students, parents, and practitioners

This goal implies that the entire education community is involved in establishing multicultural perspectives in mathematics education. I can best illustrate how this works out in practice by describing the Saundra Graham and Rosa Parks Alternative Public School in Cambridge, Massachusetts, particularly the work of teacher Judith Richards.[1]

The school accommodates four hundred students in grades K–8; about half are white and a third of the other half are Haitian American. The school has a Haitian bilingual program, and some monolingual English-speaking classes also learn Haitian Creole. The administration

---

[1]*The narrative that follows is based on my visits to Richards' classroom, which I describe in* Fear of Math *(1994), and on the chapter by Judith J. Richards, "Classroom Tapestry: A Practitioner's Perspective on Multicultural Education," in* Freedom's Plow (*Perry and Fraser 1993*).

and the entire staff are committed to multicultural education, and classes are heterogeneously grouped. A beautiful mosaic at the entrance features the two African American women who gave the school its name. Saundra Graham is a neighborhood activist and politician; Rosa Parks is famous for her refusal to sit at the back of the bus, a brave and well-planned action that led to the Montgomery bus boycott of 1956, a prelude to the widespread civil rights movement of the sixties.

When I visited, Judy Richards' combined third- and fourth-grade class had just completed a unit on Africa. The room was decorated in patterned cloth from several different regions of the continent, and other African objects, labeled as to their purpose and origin, lay on open shelves. Among them was a stack of "boards" for the mathematical game oware (see page 189), egg cartons that the children had painted in brilliant colors.

Most intriguing was a miniature compound of round houses, some molded from clay, others fashioned from tiny clay bricks. Their conical roofs were covered with foil to simulate metal. The students built these structures in connection with the following experiment: determine the shape of a house that will have the greatest floor space for a given amount of materials for the walls (see page 130). In class discussion they compared these African homes with the types of buildings they saw in their own community. The results of the experiment appeared in the portfolio that each child had assembled, along with other relevant materials, such as game boards that they had drawn for African versions of three-in-a-row games (see page 180), a good exercise in geometry and measurement.

While Judy was showing me the children's portfolios and other work, the class was busy with the "problem of the day," an algebra problem about the purchase of various quantities of East African cloth and shoes. Each group of children decided their strategies for solving the problem—guess and check, make a table and try out different values, or solve algebra equations. Meanwhile, one volunteer (the father of one of the children) was discussing the methods of solution with one group and another (an elderly woman from the community) was carrying out clerical tasks, such as checking that the children had completed their assignments. An intern from a local college circulated among the groups, throwing out hints to stimulate children's thinking.

As they carried out the study of African culture, these children were making all sorts of connections. Cooperative groups included children at two different grade levels and of various ethnic/racial backgrounds and "ability" levels. Parents, community volunteers, and college students worked with the class and contributed their knowledge. Not only were the children learning about African societies, they were also making careful observations of their own society. Their study involved most of the school subjects—mathematics, language arts, social studies, music, art, science—as well as several branches of mathematics, such as computation, algebraic thinking, geometry, measurement, and decision making.

A teacher in a classroom like this puts her students in control of their own learning. She expects that all children are capable of doing math and trusts them to work out solutions to real problems, both on their own and in cooperation with their classmates. School learning is not separate from the outside world; school, community, and the world beyond are integrated into a meaningful whole.

The Multicultural Mathematics Classroom

Multicultural education is many-faceted. It involves curriculum content, classroom management ("ability" grouping and cooperative learning groups), assessment practices, the involvement of families and the community, teacher expectations, and professional development. In the remainder of this chapter I discuss each of these facets as applied to mathematics education; in the following chapters I will concentrate on curriculum content as the factor central to introducing multicultural perspectives in mathematics education, weaving in the other aspects as appropriate.

A new type of classroom

I was teaching a class of future elementary teachers at a women's college. I had given the assignment to teach multiplication by a two-digit number to children who had already learned to multiply by a one-digit number. Each group wrote a lesson plan, and one young woman volunteered to teach the lesson according to her group's plan, while the rest of us pretended to be fourth graders. She demonstrated her procedure with a specific example—12 × 34—and then asked whether we understood. I was the only "student" who admitted that she had not understood. "Why," I asked, "do you put the 4 under the 6, and not under the 8, when you multiply 1 × 4?" Immediately the class turned on me, exclaiming, "But that's the way we were taught!" Apparently it had never occurred to them to ask Why? about the rote procedures that they had learned. The teacher was the final authority, never to be questioned.

In many classrooms today the teacher is still the final authority. She (or he) stands in front of the class and explains the new lesson. Then the rows of silent students practice by doing worksheets illustrating the new concepts or procedures, preparing for the multiple-choice test that will rank them in comparison with their peers. These students are not learning how to use the procedures to solve real problems. What they are learning is that math is dull and has nothing to do with their lives.

Ruth Parker describes the new type of classroom in her inspiring book *Mathematical Power: Lessons from a Classroom* (1993):

> Mathematics classrooms that align with the NCTM *Standards* are alive with activity. Instruction is organized into coherent multiday and multiweek units of study around rich and important mathematical investigations. Students are often seated in small heterogeneous groups, using manipulatives and other tools and considering diverse viewpoints and approaches as they work together on complex tasks. Students rely on one another, on materials, and on experts in the field as well as on the teacher. There are frequent opportunities for students to make choices and to pursue individual areas of interest. Students have frequent opportunities to communicate their findings orally and through written or graphic displays. Animated discussions are the norm as students challenge one another's thinking and present diverse points of view. Often the teacher asks probing questions designed to help students make mathematical connections. (7)

In her book Parker describes the development of one fifth-grade class over the course of a year. These students enjoyed the opportunity to construct their own knowledge, based on relevant experiences and challenges to their reasoning powers.

The role of the teacher in the new type of classroom has changed considerably. No longer does she stand in front of the class to lecture or pass judgment on students' work. Instead, she circulates around the room, observing how students cope with new ideas and throwing out hints or probing questions to help students arrive at logical conclusions. She doesn't say "right" to a correct answer or call for another student to correct a wrong answer. A child is not made to feel "dumb" when he makes a mistake. Each student is expected to justify his responses, whether they are right or wrong. There may be more than one right answer, as when a youngster is asked to show with her fingers that she would like three oranges. There may be more than one correct procedure; for instance, different methods of counting the number of grid squares enclosed by a circle (see page 130).

No longer must the teacher know everything! "Let's investigate together" or "Suppose your group does some research on that question" are acceptable responses to students' questions. From that point of view the teacher's job is easier. But assessment is much more than administering a multiple-choice test, a topic we'll discuss later in this chapter.

Learning takes time. Teachers can no longer expect a quick, automatic response to every question. The *Mathematics Framework for California Schools* states:

> *Quality work takes time.* When students are engaged in
> producing something that makes sense, with ample time to
> reflect and revise, they are more likely to succeed. . . .
>
> *Deep understanding takes time.* . . . While the idea of *mastery*
> might make sense when talking about shallow skills, the big
> ideas of mathematics continue to deepen with experience and
> maturity. (California Department of Education 1992, 38)

Cooperative learning groups and no tracking

Until the historic Supreme Court decision of 1954, segregated schooling was the accepted mode. Few heeded the voice of the noted African American scholar Doxey Wilkerson when he claimed, in a 1939 government report, *Special Problems of Negro Education*, that the differences in scholastic achievement between blacks and whites were the result of poor schooling, rather than of innate biological defects, and called on the federal government to "reverse the process and become an instrument of positive educational changes that would correct basic inequities within the society" (Dailey and Washington 1985, 105).

With the Supreme Court decision came a different form of segregation known as tracking, either by classes or by grouping within a class. In many cities housing patterns segregated children of color—the schools of the Northeast are now the most segregated in the country—which resulted in tracking by schools and districts and between cities and their suburbs. As a consequence, a disproportionate number of low-income and "minority" children are relegated to a low-level curriculum based on rote memorization and mindless drill.

Rutgers University professor Jean Anyon (1980) investigated the differences in teaching methods, classroom atmosphere, and relations between students and teachers in fifth-grade classes in several New Jersey communities, based on family income levels. It was obvious that high-income students were being groomed to take power, while poor children were expected to take orders. The least that educators can do is to abolish tracking within districts and to upgrade the curriculum, so that every student is treated with respect and has access to the most challenging and interesting materials.

Many of my suggested multicultural math activities call on students to work in cooperative groups. Ideally each group should include students of both genders, different "ability" levels, and different ethnic/racial groups. For cooperative learning to take place, the members of the group should all have responsibility both for their own learning and for that of the other members, and, of course, they should get along well together. Managing the smooth functioning of such groups takes skill and patience.

I am not suggesting that all instruction take place in cooperative learning groups. Teachers will want to use various modes of classroom management: whole class, small groups, and individual work, depending on the circumstances and the learning styles of the students. You may have to curb the individualistic spirit of some students (more often boys than girls), while encouraging others to come forth. Children from a milieu that stresses cooperation may be turned off by a competitive classroom environment and refuse to participate. Teachers must be sensitive to their students' feelings. Herbert Kohl (1994) writes about students who feel they are not respected by their teachers and believe that their only alternative is to "not-learn." Of course, another reason that students refuse to learn is that the curriculum is irrelevant and they don't see that schooling will lead to anything worthwhile in their lives.

Assessment

Until recently, assessment has relied chiefly on timed, multiple-choice tests, instruments that reward the good memorizer and penalize the reflective thinker. These tests are not aligned with the goals of multicultural education, and it is not fair to judge students' progress this way.

The new concept of performance-based assessment is ideally suited to a multicultural curriculum and classroom. Assessment should match the curriculum, consist of questions that provoke reflection and allow sufficient time for students to formulate responses, and, most important, focus on the knowledge that students have acquired rather than penalizing them for what they do not know. A good portion of assessment should be integrated with regular instruction—observing students at work, taking note of their responses to open-ended questions, and allowing them to create portfolios that reflect the work they feel best reveals their knowledge. Students should be clear about the kind of work that is expected of them and should have the opportunity to discuss the criteria for evaluating their output.

According to *FairTest Examiner* (1994), Kentucky has removed all multiple-choice questions from its statewide tests and will include only open-ended questions. After trying both types, they found that open-ended questions were a more reliable form of assessment, covered the curriculum guidelines more effectively, and removed the gender bias against girls found in many multiple-choice tests. From my own experience, I have concluded that, in general, children who are not in tune with the competitive spirit of the dominant culture do poorly on timed multiple-choice tests.

At first glance it may seem that performance-based assessment entails a lot more work for teachers. But when assessment is instruction-embedded and becomes part of the regular instructional program, separate testing becomes secondary. Of course, adopting new practices takes time and experience, and teachers should have the opportunity for both.

Schools and communities working together

When I was teaching I encountered many parents, mothers more than fathers, who would say to me, "I know Susie is not good in math, but I never could do math, either," as though Susie is now off the hook.

Stereotypes about who can and who cannot do math are particularly damaging to girls and some children of color. Parents should understand that everyone can do math.

Families are a key ingredient in children's success in school. In his research with African American families in Chicago, Reginald Clark (1983) concluded that social class and single-parenthood were far less important in explaining achievement than parental involvement in children's home activities—studying and reading with them. Even parents who are themselves unschooled can encourage their children by taking an interest in their schoolwork. The following chapters contain numerous suggestions for involving families in the life of the school and in their children's development.

Schools can interact with their communities in many ways. Here I will describe three projects that involve children in mathematics: sixth graders teaching preschoolers in New York City; a community project to clean up the neighborhood in South Tucson, Arizona; and the efforts of the Yup'ik Eskimo community to bring their traditional math and science into the curriculum in village schools in southwest Alaska. Chapter 10 contains additional case studies and suggestions for working with the community.

Children from several elementary schools enter sixth grade in Salomé Ureña Middle Academies (SUMA), also called I.S. 218 (I.S. is an abbreviation of Intermediate School). Salomé Ureña was a Dominican poet and teacher, an important role model for these predominantly Latino/a students of Dominican heritage, most of them either immigrants themselves or the children of immigrants, living in a low-income New York community.

I am a frequent visitor to the school, particularly to Gwendolyn Clinkscales' sixth-grade math classes. At the beginning of one school year, Gwen posted several Venn diagrams on the wall to help her become acquainted with her new students and to encourage interpersonal relations. In one poster she asked students to record whether they listen to the radio or watch TV when doing homework. Students were to write their initials in the "radio" circle, the "TV" circle, the intersection of the two circles, or outside both circles. The majority of the students indicated, honestly or not, that they were in the last category—no radio or TV. In another Venn diagram students were to respond to the question, How do you see yourself? The three intersecting circles were labeled "hardworking," "creative," and "organized." As you may have guessed, the majority placed their initials in the intersection of all three circles. Later in the year Gwen used these posters to teach fractions, percentages, graphs, and other topics. Students feel personally involved when the math problems are about them.

SUMA opened in 1992 as a full-service school, with health and social services for children, their families, and local residents offered through partnership with the Children's Aid Society, a "settlement house within a school." A family resource suite and a medical center are on the first floor. The school offers many afterschool activities, as well as evening courses, including English as a Second Language, for adult residents.

In her glowing description of SUMA, Joy Dryfoos writes:

> Everywhere you look, in all the halls and in the classrooms, you can find art and science projects, maps, solar systems, flying cranes, motivating slogans, a constructive and exciting environment. Recently, the entire first floor was devoted to the celebration of the Dominican national holiday, culminating with a Saturday event that drew 1,400 people to the school for cultural activities and food. One activity that I found to be truly creative and relevant involved the local police precinct in Spanish classes. The students and their parents were the teachers, who, as a team, were working in the library with the police officers to instruct them in this language. (1994, 103–104)

In response to a question about why she liked the school, one girl said: "They are respectful. . . . The people here treat you with respect." Dryfoos added: "I was impressed that she used exactly the same phrase as the principal: 'We treat the kids and their families with respect' " (106).

One of the few regular New York City public schools that does not track its students (nor are students drilled for the required standardized mathematics tests), SUMA is divided into several relatively independent academies, each with a different focus. Gwen teaches in the Community Service Academy and plans her work with the teacher of humanities. Community service for her sixth-grade math students includes working with two groups of preschoolers, from a Baptist Church center and a Jewish community center. In their twice-weekly meetings to discuss and evaluate the work of the SUMA Preschool Learning Center, the sixth graders set the agenda, lead the meeting, and make decisions as a group.

The older students read books to the children, lead them in games, and teach them math skills, thereby enriching their own understanding. For example, a large bar graph on the wall recorded—in Unifix cubes—the heights, foot lengths, and handspans of the sixth graders and preschoolers. To test which shape enclosed the greatest area, keeping the perimeter constant, they used wooden blocks to build "houses" in the shape of a square, a nonsquare rectangle, and a circle. They placed preschoolers into each house to discover which had the greatest capacity and which had the least.

After students had been given the assignment to draw floor plans of their own apartments (see page 132), some voluntarily extended their work with area, perimeter, and scale drawing into other subjects—for instance, using floor plans of Anne Frank's house to illustrate their reports on her diary. In connection with a school decision to remodel the basement to accommodate the preschoolers, students designed and drew their own plans for the space on large sheets of half-inch grid paper, letting a half-inch represent a foot. These sixth graders had not been formally taught how to do scale drawings. They developed the concepts in the course of their experience and integrated the new learning into their fund of knowledge, which they could then apply to other situations.

The plan for next year is to have the sixth-grade students design an outdoor play space with equipment for the preschoolers within the I.S. 218 schoolyard. Two architects from the Salvadori Center on the Built Environment (see page 137) will act as consultants to the classes, and a grant writer will collaborate with Gwen to seek funding for the project.

Gwen's innovative approaches to education have not gone unnoticed. She and her students have spoken about their work at many conferences, and in 1994 she received a Citibank Teacher Success Award. She was featured in *Crain's New York Business* (February 27, 1995) in an article entitled "Math teacher's angle empowers students."

In their article "Contextualized Mathematics Instruction: Moving Beyond Recent Proposals" (1994), Paul E. Heckman and Julian Weissglass advocate that mathematics be used to question societal values, especially within the context of the students' real lives. They describe the Educational and Community Change project in South Tucson, Arizona, in which students in grades four, five, and six worked with community members to clean up vacant lots littered with garbage. After surveying the area to look for patterns, the group portrayed "in graphs, photos, and maps where vacant houses and lots were located."

The children's work paid off, as the authors describe:

> In the classroom, the children estimated the amount of trash on vacant lots and compared that to lots with occupied houses. They wrote papers about the issue and presented them to their city council person and later to a community meeting that was attended by more than a thousand persons.
>
> The end result was one of the nearby, neglected, city-owned lots was donated to the school, and through independently awarded funds, a habitat for use by the entire community is being constructed on it. (31)

The children continued to work with the project. They measured the lot, estimated the amount of fencing required in light of city building codes, analyzed the types of fencing available, measured tree heights, and kept track of the finances with their own bank account for the habitat project.

The concluding paragraphs about the project are encouraging:

> The vacant lot issue took the children into the area of mathematics, as well as history, sociology, literature and civics. The combined activities of this project constitute a curriculum in real-life contextual teaching.
>
> The sociological aspects of this project are on-going. The children, parents, and neighbors have organized themselves to identify and address other community problems and issues in the hope that, over time, they can change the texture of the community. (32)

Every community presents problems that children can help to solve. For additional suggestions, see Chapter 10.

Recently I enjoyed a unique opportunity to be involved in community-school collaboration. I was asked to be a consultant in a project to bring Yup'ik Eskimo science and mathematics into K–8 schools in the predominantly Yup'ik villages of southwest Alaska. The project, which is ongoing, is sponsored by the University of Alaska Fairbanks and directed by Dr. Jerry Lipka, professor of education at the university. In his article "Culturally Negotiated Schooling: Toward a Yup'ik Mathematics" (1994), Lipka describes the project as "a deliberate process to change the context and culture of schooling." The article deals with the "possibilities of transforming the teaching of school mathematics by incorporating within it Yup'ik knowledge, culture, language, and everyday experience." He writes:

> The process of changing and negotiating the culture of
> schooling is one of collaboration with Yup'ik elders, teachers,
> community members, administrators and university faculty. As
> a result, the opportunity has been created for insiders and
> outsiders to come together to re-examine what constitutes
> school content, to value Yup'ik social processes by
> incorporating them in teaching, and to provide fresh insights
> into bridging the gap between Yup'ik ways of knowing and
> schooling. (14)

This collaboration has been going on for more than a decade under the most adverse conditions. Participants must travel great distances by bush plane in all sorts of weather. I attended two meetings of the group of forty to sixty people—elders (many of whom do not speak English), Yup'ik teachers, bilingual aides, and faculty from the university.

Among the topics we discussed were weather prediction, telling time by observing the sun and shadows, Yup'ik number words and gestures, units of measurement, geometric patterns on dance head-dresses and parkas, and the rhythms of Yup'ik dancing and drumming. (For a discussion of repeated patterns see page 149.)

Generally the elders would describe in the Yup'ik language the practices they had learned in their youth, and a teacher or aide would translate for the few of us who did not speak the language. I was tremendously impressed at the first seminar by a husband-and-wife team (a teacher and a principal, respectively) as they took turns doing a simultaneous translation of the proceedings and typing it on their personal computer. At the end of the three-day meeting they furnished each participant with seven single-spaced pages of minutes in English, with a smattering of Yup'ik words where appropriate.

Standardization of the Yup'ik number words is not a simple matter (see page 67). Besides the fact that some of the words have changed over the years, Yup'ik speakers from different regions disagree about the proper construction, spelling, and grammar. The word for four hundred was the subject of lengthy debate among several elders, teachers, and the Yup'ik professor of science education. The system is based on grouping by twenties; therefore four hundred is "twenty times twenty." Three versions were offered, but no agreement was reached.

Teachers sought interesting ways to teach the number words. A group of women put their heads together and worked out a Yup'ik-style song and dance with appropriate hand gestures and a drum accompaniment to teach the first twenty number words to young children. Some older students balk at having to memorize the words, and we discussed challenging gamelike activities to enliven the lessons.

Teachers continue to meet to develop curriculum materials and exchange experiences. However, not all members of the communities welcome the infusion of Yup'ik culture into the curriculum, and some view it as "irrelevant or even harmful to Western schooling and knowledge. The strategy that the group believes holds promise is showing the community and the school district positive evidence for these approaches" (28). Lipka's concluding statements are applicable to other communities and regions:

> Deriving mathematics from Yup'ik language, culture, and everyday experience holds promise for teaching mathematics as well as for reinforcing Yup'ik culture. Creating an atmosphere in which the very essences of schooling are analyzed and worked through with community members, teachers, and administrators can reconstitute schooling in ways that make sense for being both modern and indigenous. This may well hold promise for other groups located far from Alaska. (29)

Teacher expectations

Problems may arise as teachers try to implement both the new mathematics content and multicultural perspectives. It may take a while for students who are accustomed to the old drill-and-test curriculum to understand what is expected of them. Teachers must patiently uproot the students' view of mathematics as rote memorization, one right procedure, one right answer, and the teacher as the final authority. Happily, as students take on more responsibility, the teacher's task becomes easier.

Teachers, too, may have to change their attitudes and beliefs about who can learn mathematics. Unsubstantiated claims that girls don't have the "gene" for math, that African Americans are not capable of higher-order learning, that low-income students are not interested in school—or, on the other hand, that Asians are natural math geniuses—have claimed the attention of the media and the public. Teachers are members of our society, and some allow these attitudes to color their relations with their students. As the educator Theodore Sizer remarked: "Race and class snarl in many teachers' perceptions of students, leading to stereotypes. If you're black, you're poor. If you speak English haltingly, you're stupid. If you're white, you have a future. Blacks are basketball players. Blond is beautiful" (1984, 37).

Another unfounded belief is that students will learn successfully only with teachers who resemble them in racial/ethnic background. While it is certainly true that the presence of a more varied faculty can bring some badly needed fresh perspectives to the scene, teachers who do not look like their students can be superb teachers, as University of Wisconsin professor Gloria Ladson-Billings illustrates in *The Dreamkeepers: Successful Teachers of African American Children* (1994). She spent a considerable amount of time with eight teachers of elementary and middle grades; five were African American and three were white. They encouraged a positive cultural identification among their students and engaged in "culturally relevant teaching" that questioned the injustices that assail their students. These teachers had acquired the "cultural literacy" that enabled them to nurture their students as learners and as people.

Sensitivity to the students and their community is essential. For example, don't expect the one student of Chinese heritage in the class to be an expert on Chinese culture and practices, or necessarily to express interest in her heritage. A question addressed to the entire class—Who has seen a Chinese abacus?—does not put the Chinese student on the spot and might encourage her to volunteer personal information about the use of the abacus.

It's a good idea to try out new materials before introducing them to the class. Tracing a network, for instance, may not be as easy as it looks. I was invited to conduct a lesson in a seventh-grade class and had sent ahead materials on networks to be photocopied for distribution (see page 195). I suggested that the students try to trace one of the networks without going over a line more than once or lifting their pencils from the paper. Before they had had time to study the materials, the teacher sent one boy to the chalkboard to draw the network freehand, a difficult task even for a more sophisticated student. I realized then that the teacher had not gone through the lesson herself, and I managed to extricate the boy from her assignment.

Professional development: How can I do it all?

Are we piling another burden on already overworked elementary and middle grade teachers by introducing multicultural perspectives? It would seem so!

Multicultural mathematics education involves meaningful math activities integrated with other subjects, joint planning with teachers of those subjects, use of appropriate literature, performance-based assessment, attention to students' learning styles, and work with families and the community. Who has time for all that?

The cautionary note in the *California Mathematics Framework* is relevant: "It must be remembered that change takes time and that all elements of change must move in concert. In every school a carefully planned course of action must be adopted, and experimentation and risk taking in the classroom must be allowed. Support for change on everyone's part—teachers, parents, administrators, materials developers, and students—must be nurtured" (California Department of Education, 13). Adding the multicultural layer increases the complexity.

It's not surprising that student improvement is highest in those schools and districts that have provided the greatest opportunity for professional development and time for teachers to consult with their peers during the school year. This was the conclusion of a research study by the Kentucky Institute for Educational Reform (*FairTest Examiner* 1994). Another study by this Institute showed that students performed well in schools where the community cooperated with the schools in carrying out reforms.

According to the NCTM *Standards* (1989), "Teachers must be taught in a manner similar to how they are to teach—by exploring, conjecturing, communicating, reasoning" (253). Consider the following episode in the light of this statement.[2] One assignment in an inservice

---

[2] *I describe the incident more fully in "Multicultural Mathematics Education for the Middle Grades" (1991).*

course was to carry out the area-perimeter experiment described on page 130. Using a sheet of grid paper and a string with a length of 32 grid units, the class members were to draw a circle and several other shapes, each with a 32-unit perimeter. By counting the number of grid squares enclosed by each shape, I expected them to arrive at the conclusion that the circle encompassed the largest area. While they were working, I met with a participant to discuss her term paper.

Within a surprisingly short time everyone had completed the assignment. When I questioned them about the areas, it turned out that all the participants on one side of the room had found the area of the circle to be 95.1 square units, while those on the other side of the room agreed on 78.6 square units. They had all used the formula $Area = \pi r^2$, but one group had estimated the diameter to be ten units, while the other group used eleven units. By relying on a memorized formula, they had completely disregarded the aims of the lesson. How can they teach what they themselves have not experienced? Before giving such an assignment to their own students, teachers must be aware of the difficulties that are likely to arise.

Professional development is of the utmost importance, as *New York Times* reporter Lynda Richardson (1994) stressed in her article about South Carolina high school teacher Terry Dozier, a Vietnamese woman adopted as a child by an American family and now an adviser to Education Secretary Riley. Dozier was instrumental in shaping "changes in the Elementary and Secondary Education Act to emphasize that professional development is not a fringe benefit and should be intensive and continuous." Dozier's inspiring words emphasize the role that teachers must play in changing education:

> Whether we want to or not, we must become leaders beyond our classrooms and enable others to do so. Because until we, as a profession, accept a leadership role in the reform dialogue that is raging in this country, we will continue to be used as pawns in the game of education reform and we will never be totally successful in our primary mission of teaching.

Chapter 2

The Multicultural Mathematics Curriculum

Features of a Multicultural Mathematics Curriculum

How mathematics develops

Traditional history and literature courses have been criticized on the grounds that they deal with the exploits and products of dead white men. My experience tells me that for most young students, math is not concerned with people at all but springs full-blown from the textbook or the teacher's head. Students should realize that real people in all parts of the world and in all eras of history developed mathematical ideas because they needed to solve the vital problems of their daily existence.

The history of mathematics tells us that much of our precollege mathematics curriculum had its beginnings in Africa and Asia. Over five thousand years ago the Egyptians were using a system of written numerals based on grouping by tens, just as we do today. The numerals that enable us to write any number, however large or small, came from India by way of Arabic-speaking North Africans. The right triangle relationship known by the name of the Greek mathematician Pythagoras was known to the scholars of Mesopotamia over a millennium before Pythagoras was born. That clever calculating device called an abacus is still in use in China, Japan, Korea, and Russia.

We can't discuss multicultural mathematics curriculum in isolation from social studies, language arts, fine arts, science, and physical education. To appreciate the unique contributions of Benjamin Banneker, for example, students should learn about the situation of a free African American in the eighteenth century and the obstacles he had to overcome to attain his skills in mathematics, astronomy, and other sciences. Biographies of Banneker help students visualize life in that period. His service on the commission to survey and plan the site for the future capital of the nation in the District of Columbia involves both mathematics and American history. Familiarity with science helps to point up the tremendous achievement embodied in Banneker's almanacs, an achievement that Thomas Jefferson recognized when he sent a copy of Banneker's first almanac to the Academy of Science in Paris. Banneker's open criticism of Jefferson for holding slaves is still valid today as a condemnation of racism.

The mathematics curriculum is undergoing a complete overhaul, based on better knowledge about how children learn, the changing nature of mathematics itself, and the kind of mathematics that all people will require to function in a technological society. No longer can we be satisfied with the routine pencil-and-paper exercises based on memorized algorithms that we find in most textbooks and standardized achievement tests. The mathematics curriculum must be meaningful to all students and prepare them for the world as it is today, as well as for the world of the future. The most important and most valid mathematics curriculum is one that resonates to the students' own lives and experiences.

William F. Tate, a professor of mathematics education at the University of Wisconsin, applies this dictum to the lives of some African American students. In his article "Race, Retrenchment, and the Reform of School Mathematics" (1994), he tells about teacher Sandra Mason's class of African American students and their response to the large number of liquor stores located in their community as a result of local zoning laws. "To resolve the conflict between the local liquor laws and their negative experiences, the students have formulated and proposed mathematically based economic incentives to get liquor stores to relocate away from the school. . . . Mason has prepared them to ask and answer several questions, using mathematics, that will be important in launching arguments for their position or countering the arguments of their opponents" (482).

Designing a multicultural mathematics curriculum
Several considerations govern the design of a multicultural mathematics curriculum:

• Teachers must believe that all students can learn. They should be willing to explore such aspects as learning styles, appropriate materials, and relevant assessment procedures.

• The mathematics curriculum must engage students and challenge them to develop their critical thinking skills. "Mathematics as reasoning" is one of the main standards in the mathematics reform movement. Dressing up a routine type of exercise by placing it in an unreal story context does not engage many students, regardless of the ethnic content.

• The curriculum should promote the sharing of cultural knowledge and encourage respect among the students for one another, as well as for the members of the community and peoples of the world.

• A multicultural curriculum should empower all students by developing their leadership qualities, promoting creativity, and building confidence in their ability to apply mathematical concepts to the problems they encounter.

Learning in context

We know from our own experience that we tend to forget isolated facts. It's so much easier to remember the ideas that we can place in a familiar context, that we can incorporate into the knowledge we already possess. "Making connections" is one of the standards of the reform movement.

The *Mathematics Framework for California Public Schools* (California Department of Education 1992), a document that extends the *Curriculum and Evaluation Standards for School Mathematics* (NCTM 1989), discusses three levels of assignments: an exercise, in which the student merely follows a given procedure; a problem, which requires reasoning to apply several concepts; and an investigation, in which students formulate the problem and then apply their skills of analysis to its solution. A problem may take a class period, while an investigation may last several days or weeks. An investigation may deal with a real problem of the community, such as the prevalence of liquor stores in the neighborhood of Ms. Mason's school, or it may present a challenge, like developing strategies for a game.

Some teachers feel that students need many hours of the kind of routine drill that exercises provide, so that they will master paper-and-pencil procedures involving operations with numbers and do well on standardized tests. This type of teaching flies in the face of the way children learn. Consider how babies learn to talk, not by being taught, but through observation and the use of their problem-solving abilities. A three-year-old might say *growed* instead of *grew*. The child has learned to generalize: to indicate the past tense, add a *d* to the verb in the present tense. This kind of reasoning demonstrates a high order of thinking. Later the child will learn exceptions to the "rule." Children learn math the same way.

Children who have had the opportunity to learn in a meaningful context not only do as well in computation as those who have spent a great deal of time in drill, but rate much higher in critical thinking skills. Take, for example, the program called Finding Out/*Descubrimiento* (FO/D), described in my book *Fear of Math* (1994):

> Several hundred children in grades two, three, and four, predominantly Mexican American with varying degrees of proficiency in both English and Spanish, participated in the program. A similar number of children in a bilingual program served as a comparison group. Both groups had the same curriculum except for the FO/D activities, one hour a day for fourteen weeks.
>
> The FO/D program consisted of approximately 150 math and science activities involving measuring, counting, estimating, grouping, hypothesizing, analyzing, and reporting results. Students worked in small mixed-ability groups and were encouraged to discuss their work among themselves in English or in Spanish, as they preferred. All the materials were presented in cartoon format with texts in both Spanish and English. The children helped one another to complete worksheets in either language. . . .
>
> Although both the FO/D and comparison groups gained in math computation, a skill generally taught by rote memorization methods, the FO/D children far outdistanced the others in mathematical concepts and applications, as measured by standardized tests. Gains in all other areas were also significant. . . . Children improved, too, in their use of written

language and their level of accuracy. The outcomes
demonstrated the value of programs based on cooperative
learning groups engaged in interesting activities, the direct
opposite of the usual bilingual curriculum with its emphasis on
rote memory skills and individual seat work. (112–13)

Overview of Curriculum Chapters

Chapters 4–11 deal specifically with curriculum content. Here I will
describe several ways in which multicultural perspectives can enter the
mathematics curriculum and show how they relate to these chapters.

Mathematical topic

In chapters 4, 5, and 6, entitled "Counting with Fingers and Words,"
"Numerals: Symbols for Numbers," and "Recording and Calculating:
Tallies, Knots, and Beads," respectively, students are asked to discuss
such questions as: Why do people need numbers? How are systems of
number words in various languages related to one another? In what
other ways do people indicate numbers? What do we mean by *base*, and
how does the concept of base influence the growth of number systems?
How have people in the past written numbers? How have they used
numbers to calculate and to record data?

Geographic or cultural area

In most of the chapters I list the cultures and geographic areas to which
the various topics apply. Later in this chapter I discuss the mathematics
that evolved in ancient Egypt and how to integrate mathematics into an
interdisciplinary unit of study about this society, one of the earliest
civilizations. In Chapter 3 I include excerpts from essays and letters that
students wrote in response to their study of this culture. They demonstrate vividly that through the use of literature students identify with the
lives of Egyptians and compare them with their own lives.

Themes

In Chapter 7, "How People Use Numbers," the themes are trade and
money, keeping track of time, development of measurement systems,
and data collection. The themes are treated from the point of view of
history and of geographic region. Following this are Chapters 8 and 9,

Two Plus Two or Why Indians Flunk

by Beverly Slapin

All right, class, let's see who knows what two plus two is. Yes, Doris?

I have a question. Two plus two what?

Two plus two anything.

I don't understand.

OK, Doris, I'll explain it to you. You have two apples and you get two more. How many do you have?

Where would I get two more?

From a tree.

Why would I pick two apples if I already have two?

Never mind, you have two apples and someone gives you two more.

Why would someone give me two more, if she could give them to someone who's hungry?

Doris, it's just an example.

An example of what?

Let's try again—you have two apples and you find two more. Now how many do you have?

Who lost them?

YOU HAVE TWO PLUS TWO APPLES!!!! HOW MANY DO YOU HAVE ALL TOGETHER????

Well, if I ate one, and gave away the other three, I'd have none left, but I could always get some more if I got hungry from that tree you were talking about before.

Doris, this is your last chance—you have two, uh, buffalo, and you get two more. Now how many do you have?

It depends. How many are cows and how many are bulls, and is any of the cows pregnant?

It's hopeless! You Indians have absolutely no grasp of abstractions!

Huh?

Reprinted with permission from Beverly Slapin and Doris Seale, eds., *Through Indian Eyes: The Native Experience in Books for Children* (Philadelphia, PA: New Society Publishers, 1992).

on "Geometry and Measurement in Architecture" and "Geometry, Measurement, and Symmetry in Art." Why do people make certain choices in the style of buildings they construct? What is the significance of various forms of art? How do women contribute to the development of art forms? How does the concept of symmetry manifest itself in the arts of many cultures?

Local issues

Chapter 10, "Data Analysis and the Culture of the Community," deals with several issues that call for data collection and analysis and that provide insights on the forces and factors that determine the quality of life of a community. These insights may motivate students to take a more active interest in school activities and empower them to take appropriate action. The first activity is an investigation of the students' own heritage, an excellent tool for involving families and the community. Other themes are school finances, several environmental issues, environmental racism, smoking, demographics, life expectancy and infant mortality, and the amount of time students spend watching TV.

Games and puzzles

Games and puzzles not only are fun, they provide good learning experiences. Chapter 11, "Games of Many Cultures," helps students develop skills in logic and decision making as they solve puzzles and play games. They use geometry and measurement to design their own boards for games of position and mankala. Students learn several versions of crossing-the-river puzzles and three-in-a-row games, as well as their history and geographic dispersion. Playing games of chance leads to insights in the field of probability and combinations. Finally, the activity of drawing networks in imitation of African children's designs ties in directly with the study of networks of communications and other networks in our culture.

Grade Levels

"I love your new book and I use it a lot," said my friend about *Multicultural Mathematics: Interdisciplinary Cooperative-Learning Activities* (1993), for grades six and up. Paula teaches first grade. "How can you use a book designed for middle and secondary level?" I asked. "Oh, I adapt it," she replied.

Grade levels are not specified in the curriculum chapters. I introduce each topic with a description of the background and a discussion of the mathematical aspects, and follow with a number of suggestions for activities. Many of these are open-ended; students may carry them out on different levels, depending on their mathematical maturity and their interests. Students needn't master computational skills before they undertake a project that involves computation. For instance, if they haven't yet learned how to divide, they can use calculators. Some children will be motivated to figure out the algorithms for themselves, the best way to acquire mathematical skills.

Soon after *Africa Counts* was published, I designed activities based on African culture and tested them in middle-grade classes. Eventually I wrote articles based on this work and extensions to other culture areas; the most popular was "People Who Live in Round Houses" (1989). I often use the ideas in this article when working with teachers of various grade levels, and find that it leads to many new insights. Judy Richards adapted it to the level of her third- and fourth-grade students, and a leader in Adult Basic Education (ABE) told me that she had incorporated these ideas into the ABE mathematics curriculum for her entire state! So adapt wherever you can. Pages 215–16 of the resources list activity books and programs with a more specific focus on grade levels.

Communication

Many of the suggested activities involve communication of one form or another. Students engage in class discussions on many topics—for example, the uses of numbers in their lives. They work in small groups and plan how to carry out a project. They write in journals about the difficulties they may have experienced in solving certain problems and how they finally figured it all out. They prepare manuals to teach younger children to play games. They research topics of interest and write reports or design posters to illustrate their findings. They describe and explain their work in presentations to classmates, families, and the community.

Communication takes place in a context—to explain to others, to give voice to difficulties, to report on a topic of interest, to convince classmates to undertake a certain course of action, and even to present a point of view and urge a course of action on a legislative body or public institution, such as a campaign to remove ads for cigarettes from sports stadiums (see page 170). Students best develop their skills in speaking and writing when they express themselves for a specific purpose and audience. At the same time they are clarifying their understanding of mathematical language.

Interdisciplinary Connections

The reform movement in mathematics education is a reaction to the sad fact that much of the traditional mathematics curriculum had little relevance to the lives of students or to other aspects of school life. Mathematics was not connected to anything. Many students were unable to apply the math they learned in school to solve everyday problems. At the same time, people who needed to use math worked out their own methods of handling their problems, whether shopping for the best buys in the supermarket (described by Jean Lave in *Cognition in Practice: Mind, Mathematics, and Culture in Everyday Life* [1988]) or planning to make a quilt, like the Kentucky mothers who thought they didn't know any math and consequently were afraid of the subject (see page 145).

Teachers who are responsible for all or most of the subject areas are indeed fortunate. They can weave the study of mathematics into the context of life in colonial America by having their students make quilts and, incidentally, learn that the art of quiltmaking was one of the few means of expression for women in that society. The history of calendars fits right in with the study of the solar system and can lead to a discussion of the almanacs of Benjamin Banneker. The opportunities for interweaving the various disciplines are endless.

Increasingly, middle and secondary mathematics teachers find that their teaching benefits from collaboration with teachers of other disciplines in planning their lessons. The study of Native People's lives in her social studies class motivated a seventh grader to construct a fine model of an Iroquois longhouse out of popsicle sticks (see page 128). A model of the concentration camp at Auschwitz was also inspired by social studies lessons. Some sixth graders, after making scale drawings of their apartments in math class (see page 132), then drew floor plans of Anne Frank's attic in their humanities class, an unsolicited offshoot of their math learning in the context of the study of racism, slavery, and the Holocaust.

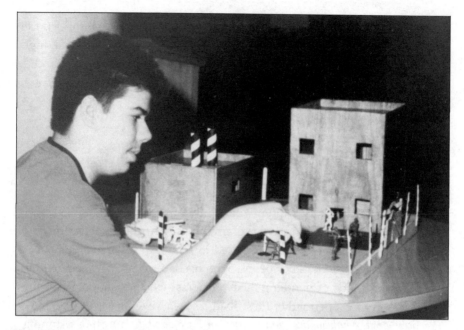

■ FIGURE 2–1 Juan with his model of the Auschwitz concentration camp. Photograph by Sam Zaslavsky

The integration of mathematics with other subjects is not easy. The *Mathematics Framework for California Schools* (California Department of Education 1992) lists the following guidelines in designing an integrated assignment, unit, or course:

1. The assignment, unit, or course should advance learning in each of the subjects integrated. . . .
2. The assignment, unit, or course should focus on curricular goals that are central to all of the subjects integrated. . . .
3. An integrated assignment should be assessed from more than one perspective. . . . (102)

An Interdisciplinary Unit on Ancient Egypt

Ancient Egypt, with its high civilization dating back over five thousand years, has long held the attention of both historians and people in general. We are still not certain about the methods of the architects and workers who designed and built the pyramids on the basis of astoundingly accurate measurements. Egyptian achievements in areas such as language development, historical writing, architecture, and the establishment of an accurate solar calendar had a tremendous influence on future societies. Some of our popular games can be traced back to this ancient African land.

Here I will set forth the mathematical aspects of an interdisciplinary unit on ancient Egypt appropriate for middle grades. I refer to the chapters in this book and to a selected list of children's books that deal with the subject. Encyclopedias and books on the history of mathematics and science are also good sources of information. Then I will discuss how such a unit can promote the goals of multiculturalism.

Mathematics content and links to other subject areas

Mathematics
- Numerals based on grouping by tens; unit fractions; Eye of Horus fractions; computation (addition, subtraction, multiplication by doubling) (Chapter 5, Lumpkin 1992, Lumpkin & Strong 1995, Woods 1988, Zaslavsky 1993, 1994).

- Standardized measures of length and capacity (Chapter 7, Lumpkin 1992, Lumpkin & Strong 1995, Zaslavsky 1994).

- Coordinate geometry, proportions (Lumpkin & Strong 1995).

Science
- Sundial and waterclock (Lumpkin & Strong 1995).
- Solar calendar dating back over six millennia (Chapter 7, Woods 1988).
- Possible relationship of Egyptian multiplication by doubling to the Ishango bone, and the problems of dating ancient artifacts (Chapter 6).
- Nilometer to measure the effect of floods on the depth of the Nile River (Woods 1988).
- Sailboats (Lumpkin & Strong 1995).

Architecture
- Building pyramids, obelisks, and temples (Chapter 8, A. Ashman 1990, Lumpkin 1992, Lumpkin & Strong 1995, Macaulay 1975, Zaslavsky 1993).

- Building homes (Lumpkin & Strong 1995).
- Scale drawing (Lumpkin & Strong 1995).

Art

- Hieroglyphics (Woods 1988).
- Mask making; symmetry and repeated patterns (Glubok 1962).

Language Arts

- Reading literature.
- Writing essays, letters, etc. (Chapter 3).

Geography

- Reading and drawing maps; computing distances on a map.

Social Studies

- Markets and barter; women as traders (Lumpkin 1992, Lumpkin & Strong 1995).
- Keeping records for such activities as building pyramids and temples, paying wages, exchanging goods, etc. (Lumpkin 1992).

Education

- Education of scribes and of the general population (Lumpkin 1992).

Recreation

- Games of position (Chapter 11).
- Mankala games (Chapter 11, Lumpkin & Strong 1995, Zaslavsky 1994).

Selected references

Children's Books

Ashman, A. 1990. *Make This Egyptian Temple*. Tulsa, OK: EDC Publishing. The book includes a cutout model of a temple.

Glubok, S. 1962. *The Art of Ancient Egypt*. New York: Atheneum.

Lumpkin, B. 1992. *Senefer: A Young Genius in Old Egypt*. Lawrenceville, NJ: Africa World Press.

Macaulay, D. 1975. *Pyramid*. New York: Houghton Mifflin.

Woods, G. 1988. *Science in Ancient Egypt*. New York: Franklin Watts.

Activity Books

Lumpkin, B. & D. Strong. 1995. *Multicultural Science and Math Connections*, pages 3–37. Portland, ME: J. Weston Walch.

Zaslavsky, C. 1993. *Multicultural Mathematics: Interdisciplinary Cooperative-Learning Activities*. Portland, ME: J. Weston Walch.

————. 1994. *Multicultural Math: Hands-On Activities from Around the World*. New York: Scholastic Professional.

For Teachers

Davidman, L. & P. 1994. *Teaching with a Multicultural Perspective: A Practical Guide*, 150–60. White Plains, NY: Longman. The authors lay out a comprehensive and multifaceted unit on ancient Egypt for sixth grade, designed by several teachers. They describe in considerable detail the content within each discipline, objectives of the unit (cognitive, affective, and skill development), generalizations and main ideas, several classroom activities, and a statement of multicultural perspectives and the strategies for achieving the stated goals. The Davidmans then proceed to analyze the lesson and offer suggestions for improving it, focusing on promoting educational equity and assuring the accuracy of the content.

How does this unit promote the goals of multiculturalism?

Expanded Knowledge of an African Society. It may seem obvious that ancient Egypt is an African society. After all, Egypt is part of the African continent, and over its long history it has had close relations with neighboring African lands. The illustrations in *Senefer: A Young Genius in Old Egypt* (Lumpkin 1992) depict brown-skinned people. The female pharaoh Hatshepsut is pictured with distinctly Black African features, a historically correct representation of the pharaohs of the eighteenth dynasty. Yet the question of the skin color of the ancient Egyptian people is controversial in both past and current literature.

Until recently many historians regarded Egypt as part of a Mediterranean civilization, distinct from Africa, and assumed that its population had white skins. The scholars who dispute this Eurocentric view claim that it arose from the racist attitudes of the past few centuries, the need of the colonial powers to denigrate the African people in order to justify the practices of slavery and racism. Students may want to discuss this question of skin color and the reasons for the disagreement. The Davidmans (1994, 157–60, 219–20) devote a considerable section of their unit on ancient Egypt to this controversy, with citations from both sides. They write: "In the case of ancient Egyptian civilizations, students should learn that over a 3,500-year period, the leaders and creators of this civilization were people of various colors—tan, brown, and black" (156). Further, they emphasize that for significant periods, pharaohs and the general population were Black Africans. They conclude the unit with this food for thought:

> At the minimum, a unit on ancient Egypt should convey that many of its pharaohs and citizens were people of color (non-White), people who were apparently much less color- and race-oriented than contemporary Americans, Canadians, Australians, Japanese, and others. Perhaps ancient Egypt has more to offer us than pyramids and mummies. (160)

Another point of historical importance is the debt that ancient Greek mathematicians owed to Egypt. It was the custom for upper-class Greek men to complete their education by studying in Egypt and Mesopotamia. Two examples are Thales, considered the father of Greek mathematics, and Pythagoras, of the famous school and theorem. Many centuries earlier the Egyptian priests had developed a complete curriculum that included such mathematically related subjects as astronomy, geometry, engineering, and architecture.

Promotion of Cultural Pluralism. The unit should lead students to conclude that people of all ethnic and racial groups have the same innate capacity and intelligence, as the preceding section indicates. Students who trace their heritage to Africa may feel empowered by the study of ancient Egypt. This feeling of empowerment comes through clearly in the essays and letters that fifth- and sixth-grade students sent to author Beatrice Lumpkin (see Chapter 3 for excerpts). For other students, this unit may be an eye-opener and encourage them to view people of all ethnic/racial backgrounds as equals.

This unit can also point up the position of women in ancient Egypt. The Greek historian Herodotus, quoted in Barber (1994), wrote in his *Histories*: "The Egyptians do practically everything backwards from other people, in their customs and laws—among which the women go to market and make deals, whereas the men stay at home and weave" (185). Herodotus was contrasting the activity of Egyptian women with the stay-at-home position of their Greek counterparts. But Herodotus was reporting only what he saw in his travels in the fifth century B.C.E. (Before the Common Era). According to Elizabeth Wayland Barber: "The male-operated vertical loom, for example, was introduced into Egypt around 1500 B.C. By that time, however, Egyptian women—and women only—had already been weaving linen on horizontal looms for fully three thousand years" (*Women's Work: The First 20,000 Years*, 1994, 186). She adds that Egyptian women continued to weave on horizontal looms and to enjoy equal status with men in the eyes of Egyptian law; they could make their own commercial deals and go into business for themselves (272–73). In my own travels in southern Nigeria I made similar observations: women wove on horizontal looms while men wove on vertical looms, and women virtually controlled many of the markets. It would be interesting to discuss the influence of ancient Egypt on other African lands from this point of view.

Indeed, Egypt has much more to teach us than pyramids and mummies!

Chapter 3

The Mathematics-Literature Connection

Through literature students can feel that they are participating in the lives of people far and near, in the distant past and in the present, in the real world and in the imaginary one. A book need not be about a mathematical topic to be useful as a springboard for mathematical investigations. Both the teacher and the students can pose problems based on the story and invent other situations by changing some elements. Not only can they ask What if? but also What if not?

In addition to the examples in this chapter, relevant books are included in the chapters on curriculum and in the resource lists.

Books for Elementary Grades

Fiction
The Black Snowman (Mendez 1989) can provide a context for discussing both African American heritage and raising money by recycling. On a more personal level, it deals with the effects of poverty and racism on a child's self-esteem. Professors Marilyn Strutchens and Fran Perkins of the University of Kentucky at Lexington use this book in their project "Multicultural Literature as a Context for Mathematical Problem Solving" to involve parents and children in mathematical activities. Marilyn obliged me by writing about some highlights of the project. Here are excerpts from her report. She begins with a rationale for using multicultural literature:

> We used multicultural literature as a context for mathematical
> problem solving. Multicultural literature depicts what is unique

to a specific culture and universal to all cultures so that it may accurately portray the nuances and variety of the day-to-day living of the culture illustrated.

She continues with a summary of the story of *The Black Snowman*:

> In the story, a snowman made out of black snow (snow filled with soot) is brought to life by a magical Kente cloth. The snowman becomes a mentor for an angry African American teen, Jacob, who feels that his family is poor because their skin color is black. The snowman discusses African warriors and leaders to help Jacob develop pride in himself and his heritage. A turning point in Jacob's life happens when the snowman helps Jacob save his younger brother, Peewee, who was trapped in an abandoned building that had caught on fire while he was searching for bottles and cans to purchase a gift for his mother.

After a discussion about Jacob and self-esteem, the parents and children in the group turned to the mathematical problems on the handout they had received from the instructors. For example, they were given the prices set by two companies for various weights of aluminum cans. Their task was to determine which company offered the better deal. Additional questions were:

- How many pounds of cans would Jacob and Peewee need to collect to buy their mother a nice gift?

- How can you determine how many cans Jacob and Peewee would need to collect to have one hundred pounds of cans?

- Suppose Peewee and Jacob collected sixty pounds of cans. How many $.05 recyclable bottles would they need to collect if they want to raise $15.00 from the combined earnings of the cans and the bottles? What percentage of the earnings would come from the cans? What percentage of the earnings would come from the bottles?

Marilyn describes the responses of the participants:

The parents and their children responded well to the story and the questions. For example, when we asked the group, How many pounds of cans would Jacob and Peewee need to collect to buy their mother a nice gift?, one parent said that it would depend on how much they wanted to spend on the gift. For [the next] question in the problem-solving section, parents and children had a blank look on their faces, until one parent said that she would first have to know how much one can weighed.

When we discussed [the last] question, we also discussed where we use percentages in the real world. We discussed how to determine how much one would pay if something was 20 percent off. We also worked on other similar examples.

Marilyn concluded her description of the activity this way:

We feel that presenting the mathematics in the context of a story that had meaning to the parents and their children helped make the mathematics more meaningful. They began to make their own connections between mathematics and the real world.

Sadako and the Thousand Paper Cranes (Coerr 1977) is another book that Marilyn and her colleague used with the parents and their children. This is a fictionalized account of a true incident. Sadako is a twelve-year-old girl suffering from radiation poisoning caused by the atomic bomb that a U.S. plane had dropped on Hiroshima near the end of World War II. As she lay in the hospital, she heard a legend that if a sick person made a thousand paper cranes, the gods would make that person healthy. Sadako, her family, and friends were able to make only 644 cranes before the girl died.

The group was visibly saddened by Sadako's fate. After they had discussed the impact of the story, they responded to questions about the average number of cranes folded per day during Sadako's illness and relevant percentages. They learned to fold paper to make cranes, a traditional Japanese art called *origami*, and discussed geometric concepts as they encountered them. As Marilyn said, "This was very challenging for the parents and their children."

In "Threading Mathematics into Social Studies" (1995), third-grade teacher Jacquelin Smith describes both the mathematical and the social learning embedded in seven books on quilting, among them *The Patchwork Quilt* (Flournoy 1985) and *Sweet Clara and the Freedom Quilt* (Hopkinson 1993).

The Patchwork Quilt tells about Tanya, an African American child, who loves to watch her grandmother convert scraps of old and new cloth into colorful patches for a quilt as the older woman relates tales about family history. Eventually Tanya is invited to join her mother and grandmother in the quilting project. Mathematical activities can range from counting the number of squares and analyzing the geometry of the patterns to making a quilt similar to the one in the story. Smith describes how each of her students measured, cut, and sewed a four-square patch of four different fabrics. These were combined into strips and then into a complete quilt. The children then presented their memory quilt to a local retirement home.

Sweet Clara and the Freedom Quilt inspired a more complex mathematical activity, as well as a profound lesson about the significance of the Underground Railroad during the era of slavery in the United States. The story concerns a patchwork quilt that incorporates a map to guide slaves in their escape from bondage. The students used tiles to form the nine-square patches, then used these as models for their final project.

As Smith states:

> The activities arising from these books encourage young children not only to appreciate diverse cultural heritages but also to develop an awareness for ways in which mathematics has played an important role throughout history. (438)

Grandfather Tang's Story (Tompert 1990) also involves geometry. Grandfather Tang relates the tale of the fox fairies and their supernatural power to change shape. The seven shapes (*tans*) of the tangram are rearranged to illustrate the characters in this folktale from China. Children can use their own tangrams to copy the shapes in the book or to create original shapes. They explore various geometric and measurement concepts, such as area and perimeter. While all shapes made from the seven tans have the same area, their perimeters can vary widely.

The Village of Round and Square Houses (Grifalconi 1987), a folktale set in Cameroon, West Africa, explains why some people live in round houses and others in square houses. Although the story is suitable for young children, it can lead to mathematical activities on a higher level, as David Whitin explains in *Read Any Good Math Lately?* (Whitin and Wilde 1992, 156–59). See Chapter 8 for a discussion of these activities. (A film based on the book is available from Weston Woods Studio, Weston, CT.)

Often the illustrations, rather than the text, suggest mathematical ideas. In *Mufaro's Beautiful Daughters: An African Tale* (Steptoe 1987), the art is inspired by the ruins of the magnificent ancient city called Great Zimbabwe, once the seat of a kingdom that extended across a large part of southern Africa. The structure known as the Temple has a massive outer stone wall thirty feet high and twenty feet thick in the shape of an ellipse two hundred feet wide and three hundred feet long. The other buildings are equally impressive. This book, both the story and the illustrations, is included in the Public Broadcasting Company (PBS) series *Reading Rainbow*.

Third-/fourth-grade teacher Judith Richards extends the usefulness of folktales by embedding mathematical problems in the context of the story:

> The practice of weaving arithmetic and problem-solving situations into the cultural folktales of the children in the classroom has allowed children of color to assume leadership roles in diverse (in terms of ethnicity, gender, language, and arithmetic skill) groups. For example, I took a well-known problem concerning the sequence of fillings and pouring with a 3- and a 7-liter container to achieve exactly 5 liters of water and weaved it into the Haitian story of Teyzen. (Richards 1993, 59)

Nonfiction

Among the seemingly endless lists of counting books, several are outstanding for their multicultural content. *Moja Means One* (Feelings 1971) teaches the words from one to ten in the Swahili language, common to a large section of East Africa, while the illustrations show interesting facts about daily life. For *two* we see two children playing a version of the widespread African game known by the generic name *mankala*, an Arabic word meaning *transferring*. See Chapter 11 for the rules of the game.

For an unusual view of counting, see *Count on Your Fingers African Style* (Zaslavsky 1980, 1996), out of print in the original 1980 version but now available from Black Butterfly with new color illustrations and additional information. Many of the thousand or more languages of Africa have very specific systems of finger gestures to supplement the number words. Chapter 4 deals with this topic at some length.

In *Thirteen Moons on Turtle's Back* (1991), Joseph Bruchac and Jonathan London use beautiful illustrations for their text about the lunar calendars of thirteen Native American peoples and the relation of each month to the natural events of the period.

Books for Middle Grades

Although books with both mathematical and multicultural content suitable for older children are generally nonfiction, teachers can adapt some of the fiction books discussed in the previous section. A good example is *The Village of Round and Square Houses.* You might use a book designed for a young audience with an older group by asking the students to make up mathematical questions that they might pose to the younger children.

The series *First Books—Science in Ancient Times*, published by Franklin Watts in 1988, consists of six books by several different authors, each dealing with a specific ancient culture: China, Egypt, Greece, Mesopotamia, Rome, and early Islam. Among the mathematical topics they discuss are number systems, astronomy, calendars, advanced mathematics, and architecture.

Students might want to investigate the history of their own families or ethnic groups with the aid of Lila Perl's *The Great Ancestor Hunt: The Fun of Finding Out Who You Are* (1994). The author gives suggestions to help students create their own ancestry charts and timelines, and includes lively anecdotes and photographs to illustrate the search for ancestors. See Chapter 10 for the mathematical aspects of this project. In the same chapter is a discussion of several ideas from *50 Simple Things Kids Can Do to Save the Earth* (Earthworks 1990).

The Story of Money (Maestro 1993) is a good introduction to the history of money for both younger and older students. Beginning with barter, it traces the development of monetary systems in ancient Sumer and other lands. Before societies used coins and paper money, they established prices in terms of various types of valued goods. Today, of course, we have credit cards and computerized banking. Readers become familiar with the cultural, historical, and political events that brought about changes in the use of money. Maps and detailed drawings of money illustrate the text.

Particular attention should be given to biographies of women and people of color who have developed mathematical and scientific ideas. Students should be familiar with Benjamin Banneker (1731–1806), the first African American scientist, surveyor, mathematician, and astronomer in the United States. Several books, at different reading levels, tell about the life and achievements of this important man, among them *Benjamin Banneker* (Conley 1989). Everyone knows about Thomas A. Edison, but how many have heard of his African American associate, Lewis H. Latimer (1848–1928), the scientist responsible for several inventions and a guidebook for engineers in the field of electric lighting?

Let's not forget the women! Teri Perl's *Women and Numbers: Lives of Women Mathematicians plus Discovery Activities* (1993) is ideal for middle-grade students, and for teachers, too. In these biographies of nineteenth- and twentieth-century women, Perl tells about their childhood experiences, their work in mathematics, and the obstacles they had to overcome. Sofia Kovalevsky, for example, had to enter into a false marriage in order to study abroad; women could not obtain a higher education in nineteenth-century Russia. Evelyn Granville was one of the first two African American women to earn a doctorate in mathematics (at Yale University, in 1949), and Edna Lee Paisano was the first American Indian to work full-time at the U.S. Census Bureau. The book includes stimulating math activities related to the work of each woman and a discussion of programs to ensure equity in mathematics education for women and girls.

Biographies of people who use mathematics are also valuable. For example, Cesar Chavez and Dolores Huerta, founders and leaders of the United Farm Workers union, used numbers and computation in the course of negotiations with employers, and are the subjects of several biographies. Another example is Marian Wright Edelman, the civil rights activist and founder of the Children's Defense Fund (CDF), discussed in Steve Otfinski's *Marian Wright Edelman: Defender of Children's Rights* (1993) and in Beatrice Siegel's *Marian Wright Edelman: The Making of a Crusader* (1995). Every year the CDF publishes extensive reports full of statistics about the status of children (see page 221). An excellent source of information about biographies of women for all age levels is the annual catalog of the National Women's History Project, 7738 Bell Road, Windsor, CA 95492-8518; telephone (707) 838-6000.

Analyzing Literature for Stereotypes

In the series of books with titles that begin *Count Your Way Through,* James Haskins takes his readers on a tour of various countries as they learn the number words in the relevant languages and the written symbols for the numbers from one to ten. However, I have a serious objection to *Count Your Way Through Africa* (1989). Although each of the other books in the series deals with an individual country, this book takes on the whole continent as though it is just a single country, thus perpetuating the stereotype that African peoples all have the same culture. The language the author presents is Swahili, spoken in East Africa.

In *Ten Little Rabbits* (Grossman 1991) Native Americans are portrayed as rabbits. Although the book is beautifully produced and has won several awards, I find this presentation of American Indian culture inaccurate and probably offensive. My first encounter with the book was in an advertisement that began: "Remember your counting rhymes from childhood? Well, this charming book takes the classic 'one little, two little, three little Indians' and does it one more. Each 'Indian' is a furry little rabbit."

This reference to the counting rhyme alerted me to danger. For many years I have discussed with teachers the negative image of Native American peoples conveyed by this rhyme. Indians should not be treated as though they were objects. Substituting one's own ethnic or religious group for the word *Indians* usually brings home the point.

Because I had not seen the book itself, I contacted Beverly Slapin and Doris Seale, coeditors of *Through Indian Eyes: The Native Experience in Books for Children* (1992), to get their opinion. In this book they list the criteria for evaluating the literature, discuss books and readings that they find objectionable, and contrast them with acceptable versions of the same topics. The criteria are also useful for analyzing books about other cultures.

In a telephone conversation, Beverly was emphatic about the offensive nature of *Ten Little Rabbits*. Not only are the characters counted as though they were objects, but human beings with their varied cultures are denigrated by being portrayed as animals. I then wrote to the *Arithmetic Teacher*, which had published David Whitin's favorable review of the book in the September 1992 issue (Whitin 1992, 56–57). There ensued a lengthy and valuable correspondence with David Whitin about this book and others. David consulted a number of people and published his two-part response to my critique in the *Arithmetic Teacher* (Whitin 1993, 114–15). Although some liked the book, others raised objections. He concluded his second letter to me: "My continuing discussion with colleagues about this book has helped to raise my awareness about portraying cultures in a sensitive and respectful manner. I thank you again for initiating this discussion and trust that our conversation will be informative to the readers of this journal as well." For a complete account of this exchange and David's further research on the subject, see the chapter "Encouraging a Multicultural Perspective" in Whitin and Wilde (1995).

A brief but informative guide is "Ten Quick Ways to Analyze Children's Books for Racism and Sexism," originally published by the Council on Interracial Books for Children and reprinted in Bigelow et al. (1994, 14–15). The guidelines include a discussion of racist, sexist, and other types of loaded words, and provide many criteria for judging children's literature.

Using literature to teach about ancient Egypt

Barbara Gathers, a teacher of fifth and sixth grades in Brooklyn, New York, enthralled her classes with two books by Beatrice Lumpkin: *Senefer: A Young Genius in Old Egypt* (Africa World Press 1992) and *Senefer and Hatshepsut: A Novel of African Genius* (now out of print but due to be reprinted). Both books introduce the female pharaoh Hatshepsut. Although Senefer was a poor boy, his skill with numbers brought him entrance into the "House of Life," the elite school for scribes. The first book describes Egyptian numerals and multiplication by doubling, while the second book includes more advanced mathematical concepts. Scenes of life in old Egypt are made vivid through the adventures of Senefer, his family, and the people of his community.

Barbara Gathers' fifth-grade class wrote about their "Day in Old Egypt." Here are excerpts from one girl's essay:

> In Ancient Egypt, in order for you to go to school you had to
> be a genius like me. In Egypt you write number one like this |,

ten like this $\cap$, 100—$\mathcal{9}$, 1,000—$\mathcal{Z}$, and so on. When I got to school there was an example on the board, next to it said "The one who gets it right gets 30 stars. . . .

The problem was

$$\cap\cap\cap\cap\cap\cap\cap\cap||\cap\cap = \underline{\hspace{3cm}}$$

and the answer I had was $||\mathcal{9}$ and I was right. I was so happy. Then it was time to go home. I told my mother the good news. Then we ate dinner. After we ate I picked more corn until it was time to go to bed.

Another day has past and a brand new one is on its way.

Students enclosed their essays in covers decorated with the Egyptian *ankh* and number symbols. One boy described his hair-raising adventures with a man-eating piranha while crossing the River Nile, only to see a mirage of palm trees in the desert as he was dying of thirst. "When I got out of the desert, there was my school. It was kind of run down but it was the best. Today we learned a new number it is 10,000,000 it looks like this ☺."

Students in the sixth-grade class wrote letters to Beatrice Lumpkin telling how the book *Senefer and Hatshepsut* had affected their lives and heightened their knowledge of mathematics. Here are some excerpts:

> The book affected my life because when I want to know something, like Senefer, I try to figure it out.

> Egyptians do most of the stuff we do in brooklyn [sic]. . . . I loved when you put math in the book. Now I know how to write Egyptian numbers, the significance of the numbers, and I learned that Math can be fun. Math is starting to be very fun and interesting.

> Three things I learned about Egyptian Mathematics was that it helped the architects when they were measuring the cubes of rock and the size of the temple or pyramid. The next thing I learned about their Math was that they had a symbol for each number starting from one all the way to one million, and the next thing Math helped the Egyptian people during their sales and to keep records of money going and coming.

> I like this book because Egyptians marry at age sixteen. My family lets us marry at the age over 25, after finishing college.

Your book has affected my view of Ancient Egypt by first of all
not lying that Egyptians are not Africans. Some people say
they are Greeks. Before the fifth grade I thought Egyptians
were Greeks, too. I thank you again for the information.

Senefer learned to count by just watching his mother write
down 2 strokes in Chapter 4. To me that shows how smart you
can be, how much brain power you have and how you can use
it. . . . Because of you I know the Egyptians were a well
budgeted country.

Your book made me learn that I should go for my goals in life
such as Senefer did when he wanted to become a scribe even
though his father wanted him to become a carpenter. I have
also learned that Hatshepsut wasn't the bold, evil, sneaky,
conniving con artist I thought she was because she wasn't
supposed to be a ruler because she was a woman, but you
showed in your book she was nice, caring woman.

The book made me just want to do research on ancient Egypt.
I say that because I thought that Ancient Egypt was dull and
stupid and just make people fall asleep, but now I know what
I've been missing. Egypt is a good place to study about.

I learned about mesopotamian [sic] numerals how to add with
them and how to multiply with them. And I also learned Egypt
numerals, how to add, subtract and multiply with them. . . .
[Your book] makes me think Egypt is a happy place because
there is no violence in the story.

Also in your book you talk about the Nilometer, fractions and
Mesopotamian numerals. I don't understand Mesopotamian
numerals but I shore [sic] understand Egyptian hieroglyphics.

For these children, Egypt had come alive—not only its mathematics,
but the life of its people. Their self-confidence grew as they identified
with the characters in the story and contrasted their own lives with
those of the Egyptians.

 *Chapter 4*

Counting with Fingers & Words

FINGER COUNTING

Mathematical Topics
Counting with gestures and words, systems based on groupings by tens or twenties.

Cultural Connections
Africa: Kenya (Kamba, Maasai, and Taita), Sierra Leone (Mende), South Africa (Zulu); Asia: India; Europe: France, England; North America: Great Plains (Native Americans), Alaska (Yup'ik), Canada (Inuit).

Background

I like to present the following scenario to an audience, whether of elementary school children, teachers, or adults in general.

"Suppose you are in a foreign country, and you don't speak the language of the region. You see some luscious-looking oranges in an outdoor market. How would you show the vendor that you want eight oranges?" Some members of the audience will suggest using the fingers. "Think about how you will use your fingers to show eight, but don't do it until I give the signal. Then hold up your hands to show eight. Keep them up while you look around at your neighbors. Are they doing it the same way, or differently?"

What a variety of ways! After they have put down their hands, I ask questions like, How many of you showed four on each hand? Did you include the thumbs? Then I ask the other people whether they showed five on the right hand or the left. Which fingers did they use to show three? They are surprised to see that this simple question has so many answers, all correct!

At a session held in a museum, one participant formed two circles with the index finger and thumb of each hand and placed one circle above the other. When I asked for an explanation, she said she was showing the numeral for eight. "But suppose these people don't use our numerals?" Well, she hadn't thought of that. She just took it for granted that everyone did it her way!

Why do people use their fingers to indicate numbers? In some cases they do it for emphasis. In other instances finger counting developed out of necessity. When people speaking different languages come together, it may be easier to use a commonly understood sign language than to try to learn several different languages.

In many cultures the practice of finger counting is as clearly defined as the number words. People would no more think of using their fingers in a random way than we would count *two, five, one, seven*. A colleague who spent some time in France observed that the French usually start with the right hand and raise the fingers one by one, beginning with the thumb. To indicate six, they raise the left thumb along with all the fingers of the right hand.

Centuries ago the Native Americans on the Great Plains invented a sign language that includes finger gestures for numbers. Counting starts by raising the little finger of the right hand, and continues as fingers are raised one by one for each number. To show six, raise all the fingers of the right hand and the thumb of the left, just as the French do. Continue until all the fingers are up, indicating ten.

I was showing Native American finger counting to an audience of teachers and university students. At the end of my demonstration, a South African graduate student announced that she would show the group the finger counting methods of her Zulu people. As it turned out, their finger gestures are exactly the same as those of the Plains Indians, except that they start with the left hand rather than the right.

The Yup'ik (Eskimo) of southwest Alaska begin their count by raising the little finger of the right hand, and continue by raising an additional finger for each number until all five fingers have been extended. For six, they raise the little finger of the left hand and touch the extended right thumb. For seven through nine, they raise two,

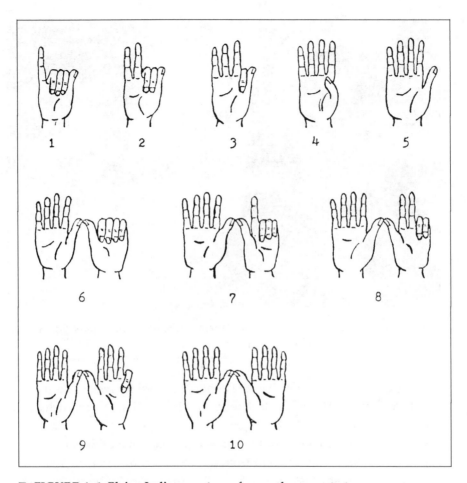

∎ FIGURE 4–1 Plains Indians gestures for numbers one to ten

three, or four fingers of the left hand. Ten is indicated by opening both hands, palms out.

In many languages number words are derived directly from the use of fingers. For example, *isithupa*, the Zulu word for six, means "thumb." The Zulu word for eight, *isishiyagalombili*, tells you to leave out two fingers; in other words, raise eight of your ten fingers. In English, eleven and twelve are derived from old English words for "one left" and "two left," the number left over after counting all ten fingers.

It is obvious that the practice of grouping by tens arose from counting the ten fingers. But some cultures group by twenties; they counted fingers and toes, at least symbolically. In the base-twenty

∎ FIGURE 4–2 Yup'ik elder Anuska Nanalook shows teacher Mary George the gesture of six. Photograph by Claudia Zaslavsky

system of the Mende people (Sierra Leone), the word for twenty means "a whole person." This is also true in several Eskimo languages, such as those of the Yup'ik and Inuit.

Neighboring peoples may have developed systems of finger counting that are quite different from one another. In *Count on Your Fingers African Style* (Zaslavsky 1980, 1996), I compare systems of finger gestures of peoples who live near one another in Kenya. The Kamba, who start counting on the right hand, show eight by using the right hand to hold three fingers of the left hand. The Taita method is to raise four fingers (not the thumb) of each hand. The Maasai hold up four fingers on the right hand and wave them.

It's interesting to compare the finger gestures with the number words. In some cases, as the Zulu "thumb" for six, they are the same. The Taita word for eight is *inyanya*, a doubling of *inya*, the word for four. The finger gesture for four is to raise four fingers of the right hand; to show eight, they raise four fingers of each hand. The words and gestures are consistent. On the other hand, the Kamba, whose number words are similar to those of the Taita (the languages belong to the same family), show eight by combining five fingers on the right hand with

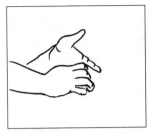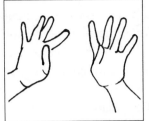

■ **FIGURE 4–3 Three ways to show "eight" in Kenya**

three on the left. See *Africa Counts: Number and Pattern in African Culture* (Zaslavsky 1979) for descriptions of several African systems of gestures for numbers and how gestures are used in different cultures.

At a workshop for teachers a participant showed the group an interesting method of finger counting. By tapping the tip and joints of her four fingers and touching the thumb joint twice, she was able to count from one to fifteen on one hand and continue to thirty on the other hand. All she could tell us about the origin of the system was that she had learned it from another teacher. Subsequently I discovered that this method was common in India and was called *angnee ka perva*, or "counting the finger joints." Counting starts with the lowest joint of the small finger, moves up to the tip, then to the lowest joint of the next finger, until the thumb is reached. Nonliterate people learn to adapt this method to perform calculations; for example, they "count on" to find the sum of two numbers, multiply by repeated doubling and divide by repeated halving.

Some occupations have their own systems of gestures for numbers. Arab and East African merchants developed a system that was understood by every trader, to enable them to reach an agreement amid the noise of the market. The same motivation inspires the gestures used by traders and employees in today's stock markets. The hearing impaired have their own system of sign language, including signs for numbers.

References to finger counting in the literature go all the way back to the *Book of the Dead* of ancient Egypt. In the European Middle Ages educated people learned how to use their fingers to show all the numbers up to 9,999. It's no wonder that the ten numerals we now use are called *digits*, from the Latin word for finger.

When I was a child it was considered shameful to use one's fingers to count or calculate. Nevertheless, many adults admit that they used their fingers under the desk, hiding the practice so that the teacher wouldn't scold. With the introduction of concrete materials, such as base-ten blocks and Cuisenaire rods, fingers came into their own. After all, what can be "handier" than the fingers?

Parents sometimes complain that their middle-grade children are still using their fingers for calculations. They should not embarrass their children by shaming them into hiding this practice. The fingers are a most basic and immediate form of calculating device. Once children have internalized an operation, they give up the use of the fingers. But some children seem to need the security of counting on their fingers. Perhaps they learn best in the tactile mode, by feeling the operation. For them, it is comforting to know that they are not alone, that people all over the world and through the ages have counted and calculated on their fingers.

Discussion and Activities

Class discussion

Ask children to discuss occasions when they used their fingers to count. They may have counted the number of days to a holiday or birthday, or the number of guests to invite to a party. Research shows that children, and adults, too, often use their fingers to calculate. I do it myself!

Role play

Suggest that students imagine they are visiting a foreign country and need to make a purchase, but cannot speak the language. Each group might make up a skit to illustrate how they would carry out the transaction, including payment for the purchase.

Generalization

Introduce the concept of a *system* of finger counting, illustrating the concept with several of the systems discussed in this chapter.

Computation

Ask students to demonstrate the use of the fingers in addition, subtraction, halving, and other operations.

Research

Have students do research to learn several formal systems of finger gestures and compare them. Perhaps parents or other family members have a tradition of finger gestures. This is an excellent way to validate the practices of people from various cultures, practices that their Americanized children may not consider worthy of remembering. Some children may be familiar with or may want to research the system of numbers in the sign language used by the hearing impaired.

Each group can learn one system and describe it to the class. Would they be able to instruct a classmate by telephone, using words only? To extend the activity, each group can prepare a manual for their system, perhaps using code letters (e.g., T = thumb) and sketches to illustrate each gesture.

Invention

Some children like to be original and make up their own system. Encourage each group of students to collaborate on an illustrated manual or poster about their invented system of finger gestures. They might extend their system to include other parts of the body—eyes, shoulders, elbows—a practice common to some people in Papua New Guinea.

NAMES FOR NUMBERS

Mathematical Topics

Construction of systems of number names, grouping by tens and by twenties, crosscultural comparisons.

Cultural Connections

Africa: Igbo and Yoruba (Nigeria), Swahili (East Africa), Mende (Sierra Leone); Asia: Japanese; Europe: English, French, German, Spanish; North America: Yup'ik (southwest Alaska).

Background

The names for small numbers were probably among the earliest inventions in many languages. Although African peoples speak a thousand languages or more, the words for two, three, and four are similar in an area comprising about half the continent, proof of their ancient origin.

Young children quickly memorize the names of the first ten or twelve numbers in the language they hear in the home, no matter how difficult that language may seem to the unaccustomed ear. Larger numbers may present problems. English-speaking children often have trouble recognizing the difference between *fourteen* and *forty*; in both words the four precedes the syllable that means ten. In the first instance, four is added to ten, while the second means four times ten. And why don't we say tenteen after nineteen, instead of twenty?

Some years ago I was asked to judge an article submitted to a mathematics teachers' journal. The author, in describing the number words of the Shona (Zimbabwe) people, wrote: "They have more number words than they need." I urged that this statement be deleted. No society has more number words than are needed by at least some members of the society, for whatever reason. Over two thousand years ago the Jaina mathematicians of ancient India devised a measure of time that would require more than two hundred digits if written out in the system we now use, a number beyond anything that most people would dream of. How many people today are familiar with the kind of numbers that astronomers and nuclear physicists bandy about in their research? Even the magnitude of the federal budget is beyond the understanding of many of the citizens who pay taxes to support it.

Every language includes some counting words. Very often these words are associated with the objects being counted, just as we have special names for certain sets: a *flock* of birds, a *pride* of lions, a *herd* of cattle, words that date back to a pastoral or agricultural society. Think about the lack of connection between the words *one* and *first*, or *two* and *second*, contrasted with *four* and *fourth*. As the society expands, as trade develops, larger numbers are needed. Rather than inventing a vast sequence of new words, the original words are combined to form higher denominations. So we have, in English, fourteen (four plus ten) and forty (four times ten), two smaller numbers connected by addition in the first case and multiplication in the second case. We'll see that some languages use the operation of subtraction, as well, to build their larger numbers.

Grouping by tens

Each language has its own specific set of number names. The important thing is that there is a *system* that allows the creation of names for larger numbers when they are needed. Certain words become building blocks, and they are combined with other words to build the system. In English, the basic building block is the number ten. We call ten the *base* of our system of number words. The word for ten is combined with the words for one through nine to form names for larger numbers. This works until we reach ninety-nine. Then a new word, *hundred* (ten times ten), comes into the picture. The next new word is *thousand* (ten times a hundred, or ten times ten times ten), followed by *million*. All the new words name powers of the base ten. In the name of a specific number, the higher powers of ten precede the lower powers in a decreasing sequence.

What a fantastic human accomplishment, to be able to express all the whole numbers from one to nine hundred ninety-nine thousand nine hundred ninety-nine using only twelve distinct words! This feat is possible only when the language has a system for building larger and larger numbers. Knowing the system enabled a nine-year-old child, Milton Sirotta, to invent a new number in 1938. He named it *googol*. A googol is written out as one followed by one hundred zeros, or ten raised to the one hundredth power. Another person did him one better by inventing the *googolplex*, ten raised to the googol power. Both these words are now in the dictionary.

To come back to the small numbers in the English language, it might seem that the words *eleven* and *twelve* are unrelated to *ten*. Actually, the word for ten is understood. *Eleven* is derived from the expression that means "one left" after counting out ten, and *twelve*, similarly, means "two left." Surely the origin lies in the practice of counting on the ten fingers.

Keep in mind that we have been describing the system of number *words* in the English language, a system constructed on the *base ten*. At this point we are not discussing written symbols for numbers, called *numerals*. That is another topic, with its own history.

Do other languages build their systems of number words in the same way? Grouping by tens is a feature of many languages. Here are some of the number names in German, Spanish, Japanese, and Swahili, a language widely used in East Africa:

	German	Spanish	Japanese	Swahili
1	eins	uno	ichi	moja
2	zwei	dos	ni	mbili
3	drei	tres	san	tatu
4	vier	cuatro	shi	nne
5	fünf	cinco	go	tano
6	sechs	seis	roku	sita
7	sieben	siete	shichi	saba
8	acht	ocho	hachi	nane
9	neun	nueve	ku	tisa
10	zehn	diez	juu	kumi
11	elf	once	juu-ichi	kumi na moja
12	zwölf	doce	juu-ni	kumi na mbili
16	sechzehn	dieciseis	juu-roku	kumi na sita
20	zwanzig	veinte	ni-juu	ishirini (from Arabic)
30	dreissig	treinta	san-juu	thelathini (from Arabic)
100	hundert	ciento	hyaku	mia moja (*mia* is Arabic)

French is surprising. Although the basic building block is ten, the name for seventy, *soixante-dix*, means sixty plus ten, *quatre-vingt* (eighty) is four times twenty, and *quatre-vingt-dix* (ninety) is four times twenty plus ten. These expressions are probably holdovers from an older system that relied on grouping by twenties, just as English has the word *score*, as in Lincoln's famous "fourscore and seven years ago."

Grouping by Twenties
Reference to the ten fingers on our hands gave rise to base-ten systems of number names. Some people counted on both fingers and toes, symbolically if not in actual practice, thus leading to systems based on grouping by twenties. In the Mende language of Sierra Leone, the term for twenty, *nu gboyongo* (or *nuu yila gboryongor*), means literally "a person," referring to all the digits on both hands and feet. Systems based on grouping by twenties are common in West Africa, among the Eskimo peoples (Inuit, Yup'ik, and others), and in the indigenous

cultures of Mexico and Central America, such as the Maya and the Aztec.

As these peoples realized, twenty is a rather large quantity for convenient grouping. They generally had way stations, subgroupings based on five and ten and sometimes fifteen. A good example is the Yup'ik language of southwest Alaska (Jacobson 1984, 668; Lipka 1994, 18):

1	atauciq	
2	malruk	
3	pingayun	
4	cetaman	
5	talliman	one arm
6	arvinlegen	cross over (to the other arm)
7	malrunlegen	two (plus) five
10	qula	above
11	qula atauciq	ten (plus) one
12	qula malruk	ten (plus) two
15	akimiaq	
16	akimiaq atauciq	fifteen (plus) one
17	akimiaq malruk	fifteen (plus) two
20	yuinaq	a whole (person)
30	yuinaq qula	twenty (plus) ten
40	yuinaak malruk	twenties (times) two

The vestiges of counting on fingers and toes can be seen in the names of the numbers for five, ten, and twenty. The term for eleven is controversial. According to a report published in 1899, the Yup'ik used a different expression, one that meant "descending to the toes." This term followed the word for ten, which means "above." Finish counting on the ten fingers above and then go down to the toes—at least symbolically!

The system of number names of the Igbo people of southeast Nigeria is also based on grouping by twenties, with a secondary base of ten. Here are some of the number words and their meanings:

1	otu	
2	abuo	
3	ato	
4	ano	
5	iso	
6	isii	
10	iri	
11	iri na otu	ten plus one

20	ohu	
21	ohu na otu	twenty plus one
30	ohu na iri	twenty plus ten
31	ohu na iri na otu	twenty plus ten plus one
40	ohu abuo	twenty (times) two
100	ohu iso	twenty (times) five

So far we have discussed systems that build larger numbers by using the operations addition and multiplication. Less common is the use of subtraction. A good example is the Yoruba language of southwest Nigeria. Here are the Yoruba counting numbers:

1	ookan	
2	eeji	
3	eeta	
4	eerin	
5	aarun	
10	eewaa	
11	ookan laa (from *ookan le ewa*)	one plus ten
12	eeji laa	two plus ten
13	eeta laa	three plus ten
14	eerin laa	four plus ten
15	eedogun (from *arun din ogun*)	five from twenty
16	eerin din logun	four from twenty
20	ogun	
21	ookan le logun	one and twenty
25	eedoogbon	five from thirty
30	ogbon	
31	ookan le logbon	one plus thirty
35	aarun din logoji	five from two twenties
40	ogoji	twenty times two
45	aarun din laadota	five from ten from three twenties
50	aadota	ten from three twenties
51	ookan le laadota	one plus (ten from three twenties) = $1 - 10 + (3 \times 20)$
55	aarun din logota	five from three twenties
60	ogota	twenty times three
100	ogorun = orun	twenty times five

The numbers between forty-one and forty-four are formed by adding to forty, while those between forty-five and fifty-nine are formed by subtracting from sixty. This method holds for every group of twenty, from forty up.

The Yoruba system seems so complicated! Yet nonliterate market women have been using it for centuries. I remarked to a young instructor at the University of Ibadan that his system of number names was fascinating. He looked puzzled, and I continued: "For example, the number words for forty-five mean 'five from ten from three twenties.' " He mumbled the Yoruba words to himself, then said: "You know, you're right. I never thought about it!"

Discussion and Activities

Discussion about uses of numbers

Discuss the many ways we use number words in daily life. How would life be different if we had no numbers at all? Students might role-play scenes in which they attempt to shop for some items, measure time or quantities, or carry out other tasks without using words or symbols for numbers.

(Be prepared for a variety of answers, possibly some unexpected ones. I was invited to read my book *Count on Your Fingers African Style* to a third-grade class during Children's Book Week. In response to my question about the use of numbers, one boy contributed a remark about "playing the numbers," the illegal gambling game that is popular in low-income communities, in conflict with the legal state lottery. The teacher quickly interjected: "But watch out for the cops!" The boy seemed bewildered by her comment, which she did not explain. Perhaps she dealt with the question after I had left, but I doubt it.)

Counting in English

Ask students to analyze the construction of the system of English number names. What is the most important number in the system? How is *ten* used as a building block to construct the system?

Can they suggest why English counting words group by tens rather than by nines or some other unit?

What does the dictionary say about the derivation of the words *eleven* and *twelve*?

What concrete materials best represent the system of English number words?

How would students go about explaining the system to younger children? They might design posters to illustrate the construction of the system.

Comparing number words

Give each student a list of the number words in several related languages—English, German, Spanish, French, and Italian, for example. Have them work in groups to compare the words for specific numbers in each language and then write their conclusions to share with the class. Can they explain why some words are similar in different languages? They might want to memorize some of the words and role-play a market scene using these words.

A group of teachers were discussing counting words in Swahili, in connection with the book *Moja Means One* (Feelings 1971). One teacher was struck by the similarity of the words for six, seven, and nine in Swahili and Hebrew. Hebrew and Arabic are closely related Semitic languages, and Swahili, a Bantu language spoken in East Africa, includes many Arabic words.

Counting in other languages

Some students may be able to count in languages other than English. Give them the opportunity to share their special knowledge with the class. Parents, grandparents, and community members can contribute the languages they know. Most people in this country had ancestors who spoke languages other than English. Each student might select one such language, learn some of its counting words, and analyze the construction of the system.

A teacher testing the lessons in *The Language of Numbers* (Education Development Center 1994) commented: "Students in my class come from all over the world. . . . [We had] students work with their families to make number charts in different languages and to produce audiotapes of native speakers counting in each language" (62).

Decoding a new language

Select a language that no student in the class knows—let's say Japanese. Give the class several number words in the language, and ask them to figure out the meaning of other words.

For example, suppose you give them:

2 ni	10 juu
3 san	12 juu-ni

What is the meaning of *juu-san*? Students should conclude that *juu-san* is the word for thirteen. Or you might ask them to guess the Japanese word for thirteen, given the list above. How do they know?

Have them discuss the operations (addition, subtraction, multiplication) by which the smaller numbers are combined to give larger numbers. They might make charts or posters to illustrate the construction.

Research base-twenty systems

Older students might do further research and analysis of one or more systems of number words based on grouping by twenties: Igbo, Yoruba, and Mende (African); Yup'ik (Eskimo); Aztec, Mayan, and Pomo (American Indian); or Gaelic (Irish).

Which operations of arithmetic are used to form larger numbers?

What type of concrete materials would best represent such a system?

What visual aids would help students to understand and use the system?

Each group of students might design a booklet explaining one specific language, and describing the people who speak it and their culture.

References

See *Africa Counts* (Zaslavsky 1979) for African languages, *The Language of Numbers* (Education Development Center 1994) for Mayan and Gaelic, *Native American Mathematics* (Closs 1986) for indigenous American languages, and *Number Words and Number Symbols* (Menninger 1992) for many languages.

SIGNIFICANT NUMBERS

Mathematical Topics
Beliefs about significance of numbers.

Cultural Connections
Europe: Greece; Middle East: Hebrew, Mesopotamia; North America: Maya, United States.

Background

When I contracted to take an apartment on the thirteenth floor of a soon-to-be-constructed building, the agent solemnly shook my hand and congratulated me on my courage. Most tall apartment and office buildings in the United States skip thirteen when they number their floors. We even have a word, *triskaidekaphobia*, that means "fear of the number thirteen." Yet the Maya considered thirteen to be one of the most favorable numbers and devised a ritual calendar composed of thirteen months of twenty days each.

In many cultures seven is a significant number. The peoples of ancient Mesopotamia endowed the number seven with special significance that comes down to us in the form of a seven-day week. For Pythagoras and the ancient Greeks, even numbers were feminine, related to earthly things, and odd numbers were masculine, pertaining to the celestial.

Discussion and Activities

Class discussion and research

Ask students what they know about beliefs in the significance of various numbers. Have them list such beliefs and try to trace them to specific societies, if possible. They might do further research by consulting their families, neighbors, and written sources. For information, see books on the history of mathematics and the extensive treatment of significant numbers in *From One to Zero* (Ifrah 1985) and *The Mystery of Numbers* (Schimmel 1993).

Chapter 5

Numerals: Symbols for Numbers

■ **Mathematical Topics**
Systems of numerals, base, place value, zero.

Cultural Connections
Africa: Ancient Egypt, medieval North Africa; America: Maya; Asia: China, India; Europe: Greece; Middle East: Mesopotamia, Hebrew.

SYMBOLS FOR NUMBERS

Introduction

We have a wonderful method of writing numbers. In fact, this system is considered one of the most important inventions in the history of humankind. To appreciate just how wonderful it is, try to imagine doing calculations with Roman numerals. How would you represent fractions and decimals? How would you enter numbers into a calculator or computer?

Our system of numerals, written symbols for numbers, is wonderful because it has three features: place value (positional notation) for successive powers of a base number, separate symbols for the numbers from one to nine, and a symbol for zero. The system originated in India about the seventh century, although some features had existed previously. Some historians think that positional notation was borrowed from the Chinese method of placing rods in columns on a counting board. Be that as it may, merchants and scientists in the Arabic-speaking lands adopted the system. Therefore we call these symbols Indo-Arabic numerals. You may have also seen them referred to as Hindu-Arabic

73

numerals, or just plain Arabic numerals. The word *Hindu* indicates a religion, while *Indo* refers to the country of origin. I believe Indo-Arabic is the most accurate designation.

Of course, symbols for numbers have a history going back thousands of years. By exploring some of these systems, students can compare them with one another and with the Indo-Arabic numerals they take for granted. Such comparisons lead to a better understanding of place value and computational procedures. In this chapter I discuss the following systems and how they can be incorporated into the curriculum: Egyptian hieroglyphics, the cuneiform numerals of Mesopotamia, Chinese rod numerals, and the Maya system of bars and dots in Middle America. Later in the chapter I introduce a game based on the Greek and Hebrew practice of using the letters of their alphabets as numerals.

Grace Cohen, a third-grade teacher in New York City, begins the school year with a study of different numeration systems. Although the emphasis is mainly on Roman and Egyptian numerals, children study wall charts showing other systems—Hebrew, Greek, Mayan, Chinese, and Babylonian (Mesopotamian). Here are some of the questions she poses:

- What are the possible reasons for the symbols for five and ten in the Roman system?
- Why do you think the Egyptians chose the lotus flower as the symbol for one thousand?
- How are the various systems similar and how do they differ?

Students design murals about Egyptian life and culture, integrating mathematics with art, language arts, history, and geography. They also form cuneiform symbols on clay tablets in imitation of the Babylonians. As the culmination of the unit, students often make up their own system, using some of the features they have discussed. These activities do much to remove the fear of math that some of these children have already developed.

Cohen also teaches courses for elementary teachers and discovers that few teachers are familiar with other systems of numeration. Her classes include people from China, Korea, and the Middle East, and they are always pleased to share knowledge of their number systems with the other participants. The students from these countries are quite facile in their "native" number systems, indicating that they have studied at least two systems, the Indo-Arabic and their own.

EGYPTIAN HIEROGLYPHICS

Background

"Accurate reckoning. The entrance into the knowledge of all existing things and all obscure secrets."

So begins the papyrus of the scribe Ah-mose, the source of a great deal of our knowledge about ancient Egyptian mathematics. In 1858 it was purchased by Henry Rhind and later given to the British Museum. Although Ah-mose (also called Ahmes) wrote the papyrus about the year 1650 B.C.E. (Before the Common Era), the exercises he copied date to a period about two hundred years earlier. Ah-mose wrote in a script we call *hieratic*. The symbols that the Egyptians engraved on stone monuments and temple walls are named hieroglyphs.

The Ah-mose papyrus has eighty-seven problems, dealing with such subjects as calculating the amount of grain needed to make a certain quantity of bread, paying workers' wages, and calculating areas and volumes of many types of objects. Some are just "guess my number" puzzles, solvable by simple algebra.

Hieroglyphic numerals

Here are the Egyptian numerals for the powers of ten up to one million:

1	10	10^2	10^3	10^4	10^5	10^6

Main features of the system

- It is based on ten and powers of ten.

- It is additive; that is, the symbol for ten is repeated three times to show thirty. The symbols might be made small to accommodate several of the same symbols in one number.

- The smallest value of the number is on the left. (Numerals were sometimes written in the opposite direction.)

- It has no symbol for zero as a placeholder. A zero symbol was unnecessary because the numbers did not have place value (positional notation). If the symbols were mixed up, we could still read the number correctly, although it might be less convenient. However, there is evidence that the Egyptians had symbols for zero to denote the absence of a quantity or the starting point of a scale for measuring.

Addition

The need for regrouping is obvious in an addition problem like the following:

$$
\begin{array}{r}
256 \\
+\ 47
\end{array}
$$

!!! ⌒⌒⌒ 99
!!!! ⌒⌒
!!! ⌒⌒

!!!!! ⌒⌒⌒ 99 = !!! ⌒⌒⌒⌒ 99 = !!!999
!!!! ⌒⌒⌒   ⌒⌒⌒

Multiplication

The ancient Egyptians multiplied two numbers by a process of doubling, a method that was still in use in Europe thousands of years later in a slightly modified form. Suppose the scribe wanted to find the product of 13 and 14:

- Set up two columns. Write the number 1 in the first column and 14 in the second column.
- Double the numbers in both columns. Continue doubling until the next number in the first column would be greater than 13, the first factor.
- Check off the numbers in the left column that add up to 13, and the corresponding numbers in the second column.
- Add the checked numbers in the right column. This sum is the product of 13 and 14.

* 1	* 14	
2	28	
* 4	* 56	
* 8	* 112	
Sums: 13	182	

The doubling procedure works because any number can be expressed as the sum of powers of two:

$$13 = 1 + 4 + 8 = 2^0 + 2^2 + 2^3$$

In effect, the procedure comes down to:

$$14 \times (1 + 4 + 8) = 14 + 56 + 112.$$

Fractions

Egyptian fractions can provide a novel approach to a topic that many students find difficult. The Egyptians wrote most fractions as the sums of two or more different unit fractions, fractions having the numerator one. (The exception was the fraction two thirds.) For example, two fifths would be written as one third plus one fifteenth. The Ah-mose papyrus includes lists of such fractions.

Eye of Horus fractions

For grain measurement, however, the scribes used a different set of fractions, symbols based on the Eye of Horus:

Note that the parts represent unit fractions with denominators that are successive powers of two.

■ **FIGURE 5–1 Eye of Horus fractions**

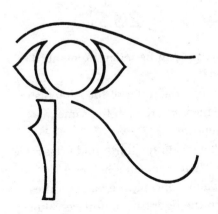
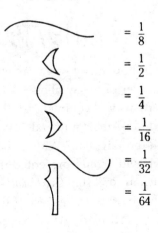

Discussion and Activities

Decoding

I like to present Egyptian hieroglyphic numerals to students in the form of a puzzle for them to solve. I might give them the following information as clues:

$$\text{IIII} \qquad \text{Ⅲ∩∩∩} \qquad \text{Ⅲ99} \qquad \text{∩∩∩9999ℤℤℤ}$$

$$\quad\; 4 \qquad\quad 37 \qquad\qquad 209 \qquad\qquad\quad 3{,}850$$

Then I ask them to decipher several hieroglyphic numerals. Of course, the examples are carefully selected to reveal the important features of the Egyptian system.

Hands-on manipulation

Students can form the symbols using pipe cleaners or similar materials and actually manipulate them. A lucky teacher in Illinois with connections to an appropriate manufacturing facility had sets of the symbols stamped out from plastic sheets. Perhaps a distributor of math materials will pick up the idea.

Place value

Challenge students to read a set of mixed-up symbols like these:

$$∩\text{II}9∩9\text{III}∩ \qquad\qquad [235]$$

In how many ways can students write 42 in Egyptian numerals if the order of the symbols is disregarded?

By way of contrast, ask them to change the order of the symbols in the Indo-Arabic numeral 421; does the meaning remain the same, as with the Egyptian? Why is there a difference?

David Whitin presented these challenges to his third-grade class. He writes in *Read Any Good Math Lately?*: "Their comments helped to highlight a central aspect of the place value concept, the value of the place, particularly when compared with the Egyptian non-place-value system. Because the children were encouraged to discover and describe the concept in their own words rather than being given a rule, their knowledge was grounded in their own thinking" (Whitin & Wilde 1992, 43).

Efficiency

Whitin suggests another way to contrast the two systems. In which system can the students write the number 98 more quickly? Students might be paired; one writes the Indo-Arabic numerals as many times as possible while the other writes 98 in Egyptian numerals twice. Clearly the Egyptian system is more cumbersome and less efficient except in certain instances. Can students find the exceptions (e.g., 100,000)?

Writing

Encourage groups of students to design stone monuments commemorating important events in Egyptian history, real or imaginary. They should include a specified number of Egyptian numerals, although the text may be in our Latin letters. They may want to write from right to left, Egyptian style.

Addition and subtraction

Once students have learned the system, they might add and subtract with Egyptian numerals. Include exercises that require regrouping. They should check by translating into Indo-Arabic numerals.

Multiplication

Pose some exercises in multiplication, or ask students to make up several for their classmates to work out. Can they carry out the doubling procedure using hieroglyphs? They should check by translating into Indo-Arabic numerals.

I had the good fortune to be asked to teach Egyptian math to small groups of fifth and sixth graders. After I had worked with them, they returned to their classroom and taught the others what they had learned. One girl was considered almost hopeless in math. Imagine her pride when she was able to make up several multiplication exercises, write them on a master sheet for duplicating, and teach the procedure to the class! This was a new topic for everyone, and she was not hampered by her previous failures.

Older students might be challenged to explain why the doubling procedure works. How might this procedure be adapted to perform division?

Fractions
Ask students to rewrite 2/7 and 2/9, for example, as the sums of unit fractions (2/7 = 1/4 + 1/28; 2/9 = 1/5 + 1/45 or 1/6 + 1/18).

Eye of Horus fractions
How are these fractions related to the procedure for multiplication? Can you find the sum of all the Eye of Horus fractions without having to add them up? How would you show this sum on a number line?

MESOPOTAMIAN MARKS IN CLAY

Background

The fertile region known as Mesopotamia covered a territory that is roughly present-day Iraq. This region is also referred to as Babylonia, after Babylon, one of its cities. Early in its history, many thousand years ago, it had already established trade links with neighboring communities.

It is thought that written numeration began with the need to keep inventories and to record transactions. Marks made with a stylus on clay tablets, called *cuneiform* numerals, indicated quantities of various items, and were perhaps the earliest records of taxation and widescale redistribution of goods and products.

Here is the numeral for 9,916: ▽ ▽ ◁ ◁ ◁ ◁ 𝅥 𝅥 𝅥

Indeed, this is a puzzle!

The Mesopotamians had two types of symbols:

A vertical wedge represented one: ▽

A horizontal wedge represented ten: ◁

To represent a number between one and nine, they made the corresponding number of vertical wedges on the clay tablet. For multiples of ten up to fifty, they recorded the appropriate number of horizontal wedges.

The Mesopotamians introduced place value based on grouping by sixties and powers of sixty. Below, the symbols in the Mesopotamian representation of 9,916 are grouped to show the value of each position or group. Note that in each group the tens are to the left of the ones.

$$2 \times 60^2 \qquad 45 \times 60 \qquad 16 \times 1$$

$$(2 \times 60^2) + (45 \times 60) + (16 \times 1) = (2 \times 3,600) + 2,700 + 16 = 9,916$$

They left a space if a certain power was missing. For example:

$$= (25 \times 60^2) + (0 \times 60) + 38 = 90,000 + 38 = 90,038$$

Of course, this was not a very good substitute for a zero symbol. Suppose the scribe or bookkeeper was careless about the size of the space. Eventually, about 2,200 years ago, two thousand years after the invention of place-value notation, a symbol for zero—two small slanting wedges—appeared. It was used only within the numeral, not at the end. Therefore it was still possible to interpret the numeral in different ways.

can mean $(2 \times 60) + 11 = 131$ or $(2 \times 60^2) + (11 \times 60) = 7,860$, or sixty times 7,860, and so on. One had to judge by the context.

To summarize, the Babylonian (Mesopotamian) system of numerals involved the following features:

- Cuneiform writing—wedges made by a stylus in clay.
- Two types of grouping, by sixties and by tens.
- Two types of symbols: a vertical wedge and a horizontal wedge.
- Place value based on sixty and powers of sixty.
- A symbol for zero used only within a numeral.

Students might wonder why sixty was selected as the unit for grouping. One reason is that certain measures consisted of sixty smaller measures. Note that sixty is divisible by many numbers: two, three, four, five, six, ten, twelve, fifteen, twenty, and thirty, making it easy to divide a large measure into many different fractional parts.

How did the Babylonians carry out calculations with so complex a system of numerals? Some clay tablets consist of tables for multiplication and division, tables of squares, and tables of cubes, indicating that they needed to calculate with such quantities.

Discussion and Activities

Class discussion

Ask students to name groupings in our culture that relate to sixty. We have sixty minutes in an hour and sixty seconds in a minute, as well as multiples and fractions of sixty, such as 360 degrees in the circle, twelve units in a dozen, twelve inches in a foot, and many more.

Translate and calculate

Encourage students to translate numbers into cuneiform symbols and cuneiform symbols into Indo-Arabic numerals. They might try to add and subtract with these numerals.

Role play

Students might pretend to be merchants and buyers and write the numbers involved in their transactions in cuneiform on clay tablets. Each group might write a scenario for such a role play and perform it for the class.

CHINESE ROD NUMERALS

Background

After the complexities of the Mesopotamian (Babylonian) system of numeration based on grouping by sixties and tens, Chinese rod numerals, also called stick numerals, will seem easy. They had their origin in the Chinese counting board, a table on which bamboo sticks were arranged in columns based on grouping by powers of ten.

The Chinese actually had four different sets of numerals: basic, official, commercial, and rods or sticks. Long before Indo-Arabic numerals became common, the Chinese devised a set of distinct symbols for the numbers from one to nine, which they then combined with symbols for ten, hundred, thousand, and so forth, to write any numerals they pleased. We shall concentrate on the rod numerals, which date to about 400 B.C.E. They are the easiest to work with and are ideal for younger children.

Here are some of the numerals. Since they follow a pattern, it should not be difficult to fill in the missing numbers.

$\mathbf{I}$	$\mathbf{II}$	$\mathbf{III}$	$\mathbf{IIII}$	$\mathbf{IIIII}$	$\mathbf{T}$	$\mathbf{\pi}$	$\mathbf{\pi}$	$\mathbf{\pi}$
1	2	3	4	5	6	7	8	9

—	=	≡	⊥	⊥	≛	I	—	I
10	20	50	60	70	90	100	1,000	10,000

The numerals above represent bamboo sticks laid out on a table in columns with headings one, ten, hundred, thousand, and so on. An empty column stood for zero. Usually the headings were not explicit; the alternating directions of the rods indicated the values of the columns. The rods were manipulated to carry out computations. Often two sets of rods of different colors, usually red and black, represented positive and negative numbers.

About the thirteenth century the Chinese borrowed the zero symbol from India for the written form of the rod numerals. Here is the written symbol for 3,702:

Discussion and Activities

Decoding

I like to present a numeral and ask students to guess the value:

$$\mathbf{III} = \mathbf{\pi} \qquad [32\mathbf{8}]$$

I offer some hints: it has three digits, place value (like ours), and each digit is related to the number of fingers on one or two hands. An alternative strategy is to identify the number above, and then ask students to figure out the value of other Chinese stick numerals.

Hands-on manipulation

Students might make a counting board having columns headed "one," "ten," and so on.

10,000	1,000	100	10	1

After they have learned to form a variety of numerals with toothpicks on the counting board, they can carry out transactions involving addition and subtraction. To add or subtract, they move and regroup the toothpicks. They should write out the scenarios for this role play.

Translation

Have students copy their stick numerals in the previous activity on diagrams of the counting board and translate them into Indo-Arabic numerals. These diagrams might form the basis for attractive posters.

Research

Investigate how the Chinese used positive and negative rod numerals.

BARS AND DOTS OF THE MAYA

Background

The Maya and their predecessors have lived, and still live, in southern Mexico and northern Central America, a region often called Meso-america (Middle America). At least two thousand years ago they were engraving their numerals in stone monuments that told the history of their rulers and other important events. Like their spoken number words, the system is based on grouping by fives and twenties. Numerals are written in vertical columns. The system has place value, with the smallest value at the bottom of the column. With two symbols, a bar and a dot, and a symbol for zero that looked like a shell, the Maya were able to denote the largest numbers. In the sixteenth century the Spanish conquerors told of Maya books containing intricate astronomical calculations, but few survived destruction either by the conquerors or by missionaries, who considered them works of the devil. Only in the last few years have these documents and monuments been translated.

Below are several numerals and their translation. The system is completely predictable; once you know the procedure, you can write any numeral.

| 1 | 2 | 5 | 9 | 10 | 13 | 15 | 16 | 20 | 134 | 399 |

We know that for everyday calculations the Maya laid out sticks and pebbles on the ground or on a table. Perhaps that's how the written symbols originated. Unfortunately we don't know what procedures they used to arrive at the answers to astronomical calculations. In one instance a date one-and-a-quarter million years in the past was calculated.

Discussion and Activities

Hands-on manipulation
Students can work with toothpicks and beans to lay out the numerals and perform calculations, and then transfer their work to paper and pencil. Can they translate from Indo-Arabic numerals to Maya, or the reverse, using only mental arithmetic?

Grouping
Students should write Maya numbers in our numerals to show the grouping:

$$= (6 \times 1) + (14 \times 20) + (5 \times 20^2) =$$
$$(6 \times 1) + (14 \times 20) + (5 \times 400) =$$
$$6 + 280 + 2,000 = 2,286$$

Research
Students may want to research the various interrelated calendars that the Maya used, and learn how they adapted the system of numerals to calculate the number of 360-day "years" between events, as well as the amount of time that had elapsed from the beginning of their reckoning in the year we call 3114 B.C.E.

LETTERS AS NUMERALS

Background

Ancient Greek and Hebrew numerals were simply the letters of their alphabets. The first ten letters represented the numbers one to ten; subsequent letters, starting with the eleventh, stood for multiples of ten and of hundreds. This is how it would work with the Latin alphabet:

A	B	C	...	I	J	K	L	...	R	S	T	U	...	Z
1	2	3		9	10	20	30		90	100	200	300		800

This practice was the origin of a Hebrew taboo involving the numeral for fifteen. Ordinarily fifteen would be written using the letters for ten and five, *yod heh*. However, this combination of letters spelled the forbidden name of Yahweh (Jehovah). Therefore the letters for nine and six were substituted.

In ancient and medieval days some Jews, and later some Christians, thought that they could predict the future or characterize a person by adding the values of the letters in a word or name. This practice—a form of numerology called Gematria—was still popular in more recent times. The sixteenth-century German algebraist Martin Stifel, an ardent disciple of the religious reformer Martin Luther, "proved" by the use of Gematria that Pope Leo X was the "beast" in the Bible by showing that the value of his name was 666. Subsequently, opponents of Martin Luther used similar reasoning to show that he, indeed, was the beast!

(A Jewish participant in a course on multicultural mathematics decided to do a research project on Gematria. Her comment when she chose the topic was interesting: "When I deal with my own culture, I consider such practices a relevant aspect of the culture. But for other societies, I would call such beliefs superstitions.")

Discussion and Activities

Numbers and letters game
Students might follow the ancient Greek and Hebrew practice, using the letters of our (Latin) alphabet. A somewhat simpler system is to number

the letters consecutively from one to twenty-six. Make up sample exercises:

What is the number for the word *dog*?

Calculate the number for your name.

Write as many words as possible that add up to 25.

Name a three-letter word that has the smallest possible value or the largest possible value.

Tell the students the number of a word and the number of letters, but omit one or two letters; for example, BE __ D = 12 [BEAD].

Ask students to invent other problems to challenge their classmates.

INDO-ARABIC NUMERALS IN EUROPE

Background

Students might wonder why centuries elapsed after the introduction of Indo-Arabic numerals in Europe before they replaced Roman numerals. In the ninth century an Arabic manuscript by the mathematician al-Khwarizmi, a member of the Cairo House of Wisdom, spread knowledge about these Indian numerals. In 1202 Leonardo of Pisa, an Italian, wrote a book in Latin in which he explained the methods of computation that he had learned from Arabic-speaking scholars in North Africa. But it was not clear sailing for the system that much of the world uses today. Merchants were afraid that a numeral might be changed with the stroke of a pen, like changing a 1 to a 7. Furthermore, the Catholic Church frowned upon the work of "infidels," as they considered Muslims. But with the growth of trade in the fifteenth century, and the availability of paper, the advantages of the new system for carrying out calculations became obvious.

Students should understand that many societies did not require extensive systems of numerals until fairly recently (historically speaking). When they needed them, they generally adopted the Indo-Arabic system.

Discussion and Activities

Research
Look up and discuss the history of Indo-Arabic numerals.

Analysis
Students might criticize the following questions and answers about the Igbo (Nigeria) system of number *words*, which is based on grouping by twenties. They appeared in a third-grade lesson of a mathematics program.

> Question: How is the Igbo [Nigeria] name for 21 different from our name for 21?
>
> Answer: The Igbo system uses words; we use numbers.
>
> Question: How is the Igbo system like our system? How does it differ?
>
> Answer: Patterns are evident in both systems. The Igbo system does not use place value.

Evidently the writer of this lesson saw no difference between a system of number *words* and a system of number *symbols*! Both the Igbo and the English number names form well-developed, logical systems, each based on its own specific type of grouping. The Igbo people write and operate computers using Indo-Arabic numerals, just as we do.

Comparison
Most important of all is to compare some of the systems we have discussed with the Indo-Arabic system. The summary on page 89 should be helpful. "Additive" refers to the repetition of symbols in a position, such as five Chinese rods in the tens place to show fifty.

Feature	Indo-Arabic	Egyptian	Chinese	Mesopo-tamian	Maya
Place value	yes	no	yes	yes	yes
Base	ten	ten	ten	sixty	twenty
Other grouping			five	ten	five
Smallest value	on right	on left	on right	on right	at bottom
Symbols	zero to nine	powers of ten	rods	wedges	bar, dot, and shell
Zero symbol	yes	no	yes	yes	yes
Additive	no	yes	yes	yes	yes

Research

One interesting project is to trace the development of Indo-Arabic numerals as they traveled from one culture to another. Even today more than one version is in use.

Another research project is an investigation of the standard Chinese numerals and a comparison of the Chinese system with the Indo-Arabic.

Invent a system

As a summation of all they have learned about systems of numerals, students might want to invent their own systems and ask their classmates to decipher and evaluate them.

Chapter 6

Recording & Calculating: Tallies, Knots, & Beads

Tallies on bones and wood, knots in grass and string, and beads on cords and wires have all had a place in recording and calculating with numbers. This chapter briefly reviews some aspects of the subject and suggests ways to involve students in hands-on activities.

■ **Mathematical Topics**
Counting, place value, computation, combinations, logical thinking.

Cultural Connections
Africa (ancient); Asia: China, Japan, Korea; Europe: Rome (ancient), Russia; North America: United States (contemporary); South America: Peru (Inca).

Linked Subjects
Archaeology, coding

TALLY MARKS ON THE ISHANGO BONE

Background

The Ishango bone is one of the most fascinating and controversial of archaeological discoveries. Many millennia ago, the people of the site now called Ishango, on the shore of Lake Rutanzige in eastern Zaire, made tools for fishing and hunting. In the 1950s the Belgian archaeologist Jean de Heinzelin unearthed a number of tools that were unlike those from other African sites. Among them was a bone tool-handle marked in notches arranged in definite patterns, with a bit of quartz still fixed at its head (see Figure 6–1). De Heinzelin thought at the time that the incised bone was about 9,000 years old, a date that has since been revised, on the basis of more recent excavations, to about 20,000 B.C.E. (Before the Common Era) or even earlier.

To de Heinzelin the notches indicated a set of prime numbers and doubling of numbers. Here is the description, quoted from *Africa Counts: Number and Pattern in African Culture* (Zaslavsky 1979):

> There are three separate columns, each consisting of sets of notches arranged in distinct patterns. One column has four groups composed of eleven, thirteen, seventeen, and nineteen notches; these are the prime numbers between ten and twenty. In another column the groups consist of eleven, twenty-one, nineteen, and nine notches, in that order. The pattern here

▮ **FIGURE 6–1 Two views of the Ishango bone**

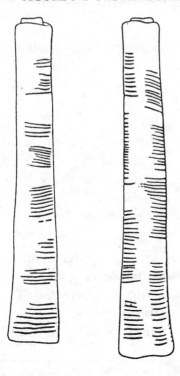

may be 10 + 1, 20 + 1, 20 − 1, and 10 − 1. The third column has the notches arranged in eight groups, in the following order: 3, 6, 4, 8, 10, 5, 5, 7. The 3 and the 6 are close together, followed by a space, then the 4 and the 8, also close together, then another space, followed by 10 and two 5's. This arrangement seems to be related to the operation of doubling. De Heinzelin concludes that the bone may have been the artifact of a people who used a number system based on ten, and who were also familiar with prime numbers and the operation of duplication. (18)

Subsequently Alexander Marshack examined the markings by microscope and came to a different conclusion. The marks were made by about thirty-nine different points, apparently at different times. He plotted the notches on the Ishango bone against a lunar model and found a close correlation. Here is possible evidence of sequential notation based on a lunar calendar for a period of almost six months. In his book *The Roots of Civilization*, Marshack (1991) discusses notational systems of similar age found in other parts of the world.

Discussion and Activities

Analysis
Students can pretend to be amateur archaeologists faced with the problem of interpreting the markings on the bone. Distribute the sketches of the Ishango bone and tell them the background, but not the interpretations by de Heinzelin or Marshack. Suggest that they count the notches in each group. (If that is too difficult, write the number next to each group before making copies of the sketches.) Can they see the relationship among the different groups of notches that de Heinzelin described? Which ancient society [Egypt] carried out multiplication by doubling?

Decision making
After they have discussed their own conclusions and compared them with those of de Heinzelin, inform them about Marshack's interpretation. Can they see any justification for it? The period of the moon's cycle is about twenty-nine and a half days. Looking at one view of the bone and adding the appropriate numbers two at a time, one

obtains four different sums of thirty, the approximate length of a lunar month: 11 + 19, 21 + 9, 11 + 19 (again), and 13 + 17.

Further research

Another aspect of archaeological research is the problem of dating. Further research at the site in the 1980s led scientists to date the Ishango bone to a period thousands of years earlier than the date originally proposed. Students might investigate dating methodology.

Role play and writing

Students may want to role-play a presentation to a meeting of a scientific society or to write a newspaper article presenting their findings.

MODERN TALLIES

Background

Records in the form of tallies have been used the world over. According to British law, records of taxes were kept on tally sticks, a practice that continued from the twelfth century until 1826. As Charles Dickens tells the story, an order was finally given to burn them in a stove in the House of Lords. Unfortunately, the hot stove set fire to the paneling, which then set fire to the House of Commons. The two houses were reduced to ashes.

Tally marks are still in use in our technological culture. Look at bar codes on grocery and other items and at postal codes on the return envelopes we receive from business establishments and charitable organizations. With the postal zones encoded on the envelopes, machines can read and sort the mail, saving a great deal of time.

Each digit is represented by a combination of five long and short marks. Here is the nine-digit code on the return envelope of the Children's Defense Fund in Baltimore, Maryland 21298-9642:

Ignore the first and last bars. The tenth digit is the checking number, and can also be ignored for our purposes.

The codes for the digits zero to nine are:

| 0 | 1 | 2 | 3 | 4 | 5 | 6 | 7 | 8 | 9 |

Discussion and Activities

Class discussion

Ask students whether they have seen tally marks in their environment. Discuss the use of tallies in our culture and the ease with which a computer can read the codes at the checkout counter or the post office. They might bring in some examples.

Decoding postal codes

Postal codes are easier to read than bar codes. Give students some simple examples to decode, such as the following old-fashioned five-digit zip codes:

19005

10468

21297

80327

They should notice that each code has five digits and twenty-five symbols. By matching the symbols for the various digits, they should be able to construct a chart of symbols for the digits zero to nine.

Arrangements

Students should note that each symbol consists of two long and three short marks. Would some other combination of long and short tallies work as well? Three long and two short would also work. They might write out, in an orderly way, all possible arrangements of long and short marks, and count them. Combinations of one long and four short, or four long and one short, would permit only five digits. Ask students to justify their conclusions.

Analysis

Ask the students to examine their lists of symbols for 0 to 9. Are any additional combinations of two long and three short marks possible? Challenge them to prove that exactly ten arrangements, and only ten, can be formed.

Practice

Bring in coded envelopes for students to decode, or ask them to bring in such envelopes. Conceal the zip codes expressed in standard numerals, and ask students to figure them out. They can check by referring to the numerals. For ease in matching the marks to their key, they might chant in rhythm: for example, "Lo-ong, short, short, lo-ong, short."

Invention

Challenge students to invent their own codes based on tally marks. Can they improve upon the postal system?

KNOTS IN STRING: THE INCA QUIPU

Background

Every ten years the United States conducts a census of its inhabitants. From this census the Census Bureau constructs tables describing many features of life in this country—income, educational levels, number of cars and television sets, and lots more. The census figures also form the basis for the funds that the federal government allots to the cities and states for educational, health, and other programs.

The government of the Incas (also spelled Inka) also kept elaborate records. From about the years 1400 to 1540 the Incas controlled a vast area along the west coast of South America. They imposed their institutions of government on the peoples they governed but allowed these peoples to maintain their own cultures. Cuzco, the capital, was situated at an elevation of 11,000 feet in the land that is now Peru. The common language was Quechua, still in use today, but many different languages were spoken by the peoples of the subject lands.

The Incas maintained their control through elaborate systems of roads and information gathering. Well-trained officials in each region, as well as in the capital, kept accurate records (of things like number of people, product amounts, and tax levies) encoded in *quipus*. A quipu (KEE poo) is a collection of strings of several different colors in which the official makes knots to indicate various quantities. It has been called a "tangled mop." The knots in each string indicate a certain number in a base-ten place-value system. The strings could be detached easily for updating. Swift messengers carried them along the highways from the provinces to Cuzco and back.

Fig. 6–2 is a diagram of a simple quipu. The first string shows 314, the second shows 23, and the third shows 105. The top string shows the sum of the lower strings, 442. Note that the empty space denotes zero in our numerals. Actual quipus used a different type of knots in the units

▮ **FIGURE 6–2 Quipu diagram**

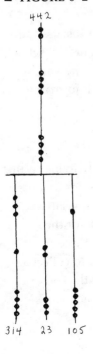

place, so that there could be no confusion in reading the number. See *Code of the Quipu* (Ascher and Ascher 1981) and *Ethnomathematics* (Ascher 1991) for beautiful descriptions of quipus and quipu makers and how they functioned in Inca society.

A word of caution is in order here. Several books and articles show quipus in which each string represents a different place value, similar to an abacus. This would make the quipu very cumbersome and hard to read. In practice, each quantity was recorded on one cord. The color and placement of the cords furnished the key to the various types of data.

Many societies have used knots in fiber to keep track of time, to record quantities, and for other purposes. A young man living on the slopes of Mount Kilimanjaro in Tanzania was about to set out on a twelve-day journey. To help his wife keep track of the days, he tied twelve knots in a length of banana plant fiber. Every day she untied one knot as she awaited his homecoming. In another African culture a man would tie knots in two strings, one for himself and the other for his wife (see *Africa Counts*, Zaslavsky 1979).

Discussion and Activities

Class discussion

Ask students how they remember important events. Then discuss the types of information that are necessary to run the classroom, the school, and the home. How is this information collected? How do the various levels of government collect information, and how is this information used?

Role play

Have each group of students pretend that they are a family living in the Andes Mountains of South America. They freeze-dry potatoes to store for the future. (The potato plant originated in this region and later became a staple crop in Europe and elsewhere. At the time of the Spanish conquest, Andean farmers were producing about three thousand varieties of potato.) The local government needs to collect a record of each family's consumption of potatoes for a month. Each group should first make a table of their consumption for each week, then transfer the quantities to a diagram of a quipu.

Make a quipu

Ambitious students might take on the character of the quipu makers and devise real quipus. They might either make knots in the cords or knot small beads onto the cord. Can they carry out the addition mentally, as the quipu makers may have done?

Comparisons

Students should compare the collection and recording of data on quipus with our methods of collecting and recording data—telephone, fax, paper and pencil, computers, etc.—to make them aware of the tremendous advances in communication since the days of the Inca.

U. S. Census

Older students can learn about the census conducted every ten years. See *Counting America* (Ashabranner & Ashabranner 1989). They might discuss taking a census in the classroom, the school, or the community.

BEADS ON THE ABACUS

Background

People wonder how the Romans were able to calculate with their numerals. They didn't, not in the sense that we calculate with Indo-Arabic numerals. The Romans and other people used counting boards. This practice continued for many centuries.

We have discussed Chinese rod numerals, originally actual sticks laid out and manipulated on a counting board. Eventually, about eight centuries ago, someone had the bright idea to string beads on cords and attach them to a frame. The result was the *suan pan*, which means "counting board" (see Fig. 6–3).

The arrangement on the *suan pan* is similar to that of Chinese rods on a counting board (see page 83). Each strand has a value that is ten times the value of the strand to its right. The *suan pan* uses a place-value system based on grouping by tens and powers of ten. As with the rod numerals, groups of five are also used. In each position the beads below the crossbar represent units from one to five. Each of the two beads above the crossbar represents a group of five.

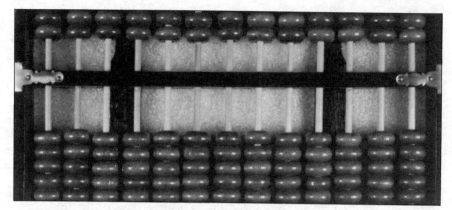

∎ FIGURE 6–3 Suan pan. Photographs by Sam Zaslavsky

To record the number 5,072, for example:

- Start at the far right strand. Push two beads in the lower section toward the crossbar to record the 2 in the units place.
- On the second strand from the right, push two lower beads and one upper bead toward the crossbar to record $2 + 5 = 7$ in the tens place.
- Leave the third strand untouched to indicate zero in the hundreds place.
- On the fourth strand, push one upper bead toward the crossbar to record 5 in the thousands place.

Now use the abacus to add 8 to 5,072:

- Think of 8 as 3 + 5. On the far right strand, push the remaining three lower beads toward the crossbar to record the addition of 3. The abacus shows 5,075.

- On the same strand, exchange the five lower beads for one upper bead. Push the lower beads down toward the frame. Push one upper bead toward the crossbar. The abacus now shows 5,075 a different way.

- On the same strand, add another five by pushing the second upper bead toward the crossbar. The abacus shows 5,070, plus 10 in the units place, for a total of 5,080.

- Exchange the two fives in the units place for one ten in the tens place. Push the two upper beads on the far right strand up to the frame. On the tens strand push another lower bead toward the crossbar. The abacus shows 5,080.

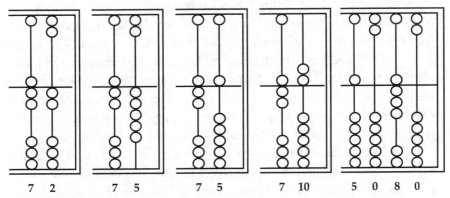

| 7 | 2 | | 7 | 5 | | 7 | 5 | | 7 | 10 | | 5 | 0 | 8 | 0 |

For a detailed lesson on making and using a Chinese abacus and a discussion of the mathematical aspects, see *The Language of Numbers* (Education Development Center 1994), pages 22–31.

The Japanese adopted the Chinese abacus, and, with their well-known efficiency, improved it so that fewer beads needed to be moved. In the abacus of Fig. 6–4, called the *soroban*, each strand has just four beads below the crossbar and one bead above it. The soroban in the illustration shows 5,072. Students might discuss how to add 8 to that number on the soroban.

The *suan pan* and the *soroban* are still in use and can be purchased in

■ **FIGURE 6–4 Soroban shows 5,072. Photograph by Sam Zaslavsky**

the United States. It might seem that pushing beads on an abacus is slower than using a calculator. However, in contests between calculator operators and users of the abacus, the abacus was faster for addition and subtraction. People who use the abacus learn to do many operations mentally. In fact, Japanese children learn to use the abacus along with pencil-and-paper methods of calculation.

In the 1970s, Hang Young Pai, a Korean mathematician, introduced to the United States a method of calculating on the fingers that his father had invented in Korea. He called it *Chisanbop*; it is also known as *Fingermath*.™ The basis for the method is the Korean abacus, which is identical to the soroban. The four fingers are equivalent to the four lower beads on the soroban, and the thumb represents five. Counting and calculating start with the right hand, representing the units place, while the left hand indicates the number of tens.

The Russian abacus (Fig. 6–5), called a *scety* (s'CHAW tee), from the Russian word "to count," may be easier for American children to use. Perhaps they played with a similar device when they were small. Such devices were probably modeled on the *scety*. When the French invaded Russia in 1812, a French mathematician noticed that Russians were using this abacus. He thought it was a wonderful way for children to learn arithmetic, and brought the idea back to France. From there it spread to other European countries and to America. Even today, a *scety* often lies next to the cash register in Russian shops. The simplified *scety* illustrated here shows 5,072.03, and is handy for computing dollars and cents. Note that the two middle beads on each strand are darker, to facilitate counting the beads. The decimal point is indicated by a strand with a single bead. To record a number, slide the appropriate number of beads from right to left.

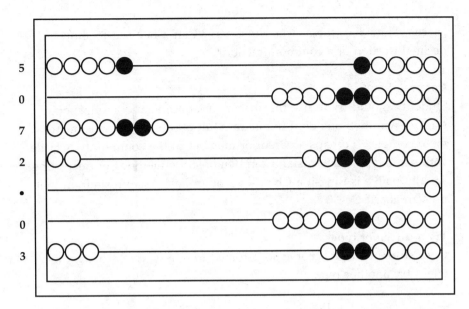

■ **FIGURE 6–5** Scety shows 5,072.03.

Discussion and Activities

Using an abacus

Children should have access to at least one type of abacus, or they can make their own. The abacus provides an excellent way to reinforce concepts of place value and regrouping. Both the Russian and the Chinese devices permit a number to be shown in more than one way. For example, to show ten on the *scety*, either slide ten beads on the units strand to the left, or just one bead on the tens strand. Here are three ways to show ten on the *suan pan*: on the units strand move five lower beads and one upper bead; or move two upper beads; or move one lower bead on the tens strand. Why is it not possible to show ten in more than one way on the *soroban*? Ask students to carry out all the possibilities discussed here, either on an abacus or by making diagrams.

Comparison with standard numerals

Basic to any series of lessons with an abacus is to relate it to our base-ten place-value system of numerals. Discuss similarities and differences. Students should recognize that both systems use place value. For example, in the number 5,072, the digit for 5 in the thousands place means five times one thousand, or five thousand. How does the abacus show five thousand? That depends to some extent on the type of abacus. How does the abacus show zero? Can it be used to show a decimal fraction or a common fraction?

Computation

Students should try to use the abacus for addition and subtraction, starting with two one-digit numbers. Multiplication and division are more complex. Perhaps a parent or member of the community is facile with some type of abacus and can demonstrate methods of calculating. An alternative is to visit a Chinese or other East Asian restaurant that uses an abacus.

Try a different type

Once students have become accustomed to one type of abacus, they might try another type.

Teaching young children

A good exercise is for each group to make a simple abacus with two or three strands, write and illustrate a manual for its use, and teach a group of younger children the skills they have acquired.

Research and invention

Ambitious students may want to research other types of counting devices. Perhaps they will learn the *Chisanbop* method of finger calculation. Or they might invent an abacus to accommodate the Maya base-twenty system of numeration, with subgroups of fives. I actually saw a photograph of such an abacus, from the collection in a Portuguese museum, but was unable to learn more about it. It consisted of a number of horizontal strands with a divider down the middle. On each cord were four beads on one side of the divider and three beads on the other side. The cords were attached to a cloth or leather wrapping, which could then be rolled up for ease in carrying.

Chapter 7

How People Use Numbers

Theme
Use of numbers in such universal activities as trading, keeping track of time, measuring objects, and collecting data.

Mathematical Topics
Computation, mental arithmetic, equivalence, estimation, measurement systems.

Cultural Connections
Africa: Ancient Egypt, West Africa (ancient Ghana and Mali, Asante, Nigeria), Congo; Asia: Ancient Mesopotamia, India, China, Turkey (ancient Lydia), Japan, Islamic, Jewish; Europe: Spain, Norse (Viking); America: Iroquois, Aztec, Maya.

Linked Subjects
Astronomy, timekeeping.

TRADE, MONEY, AND MENTAL ARITHMETIC

Background

A long time ago the people of a community made or grew all the things they needed without having to buy or sell. Perhaps a farmer exchanged a sack of corn for an axe or a sheepskin pelt. Or the village might exchange wool from their sheep for the pots made in another village. This system of exchange is called barter. In some rural areas barter is still the main method of trading.

Eventually trade grew to the point where barter was not convenient. Then people began to use money. At the same time, they didn't want to give up the idea of useful exchange. The early forms of money were objects that people could use in rituals, for decoration, or as part of everyday life—beads, cowrie shells, textiles, metal objects. For example, the Iroquois (American Indians) of the Northeast used shell beads, called *wampum*, to design belts that incorporated messages or treaties. Only later did they exchange strings of wampum for furs with the European colonists. Wampum became the common currency for both the native peoples and the colonists.

(Some of these exchanges were disastrous for the indigenous peoples. Europeans regarded land as a commodity that could be bought and sold, while the Indians believed that land was held in common for the use of all the people of the group. They did not realize that they were giving up the right to use the land when they accepted gifts from the Europeans. A notable example is the "sale" of the island of Manhattan to the Dutch by the Manhatta Indians in 1626.)

Cowrie shells were a popular form of currency in India, China, and other Asian countries, as well as in regions of Africa. The ancient Egyptians considered the cowrie a magic token, a symbol of fertility, and they occasionally used cowries in foreign exchange. In trade with Europeans, Africans often expressed a preference for cowries rather than gold as payment for commodities. Cowries were, and still are, used as decorative objects, as game pieces, and in many other ways. In the fourteenth century the North African traveler Ibn Battuta reported that one gold dinar (an Arabic coin) was worth 1,150 cowries in the West African regions of Gao and Mali. Even into the twentieth century, cowries were handy for small purchases. In parts of West Africa, forty cowrie shells were strung in a sort of necklace, called a *string*. I purchased such a string in Nigeria in 1974, forty shells on several strands of grass. Five strings formed a *bunch*, ten bunches were a *head*, and ten heads (20,000 shells) were a *bag*, as much as a man could carry on his head. In some areas where French traders held sway, a bag was known as a *captif*, a captive, a reference to the nefarious slave trade.

Europeans were amazed by the skill in mental arithmetic displayed by African traders, both women and men. In parts of West Africa it was the women who dominated commerce. African merchants could do complex arithmetic in their heads and remember sales figures for years.

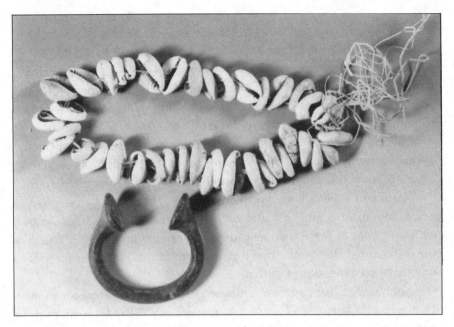

■ FIGURE 7–1 Cowrie shell and manilla currency. Photograph by Sam Zaslavsky

At the time the Spanish conquerors invaded Mexico in 1519, the Aztecs were using cocoa beans as currency. In this culture, 8,000 beans were considered a *bag*. The Aztec numeration system, like that of the Maya, was based on grouping by twenties.

The first coins were actually lumps of metal with simple designs. As far as we know, the first coins appeared in Lydia, now part of Turkey, about 2,600 years ago. Other forms of metal currency might be shaped like tools or animals, as in Japan and China. For centuries, copper bracelets called *manillas* (Portuguese for bracelet) were the most celebrated currency in the Niger River delta (now Nigeria), and varied in weight from three ounces to six pounds. Eventually five different sizes became standard in various parts of the region. The metal might be used later to manufacture other useful objects.

In the year 951 the king of the ancient West African kingdom of Ghana (north of modern Ghana) was considered the wealthiest man in the world. Somewhat later, in 1324, Mansa Musa, the ruler of the West African kingdom of ancient Mali, undertook the traditional Muslim pilgrimage to Mecca, traveling with 60,000 men and such a huge quantity of gold that the value of the Egyptian *dinar* was depressed for twelve years afterward. East Africa was the main source of gold for Asia, while the gold mines of West Africa were the basis for much of Europe's currency until the sixteenth century, when Europeans learned about the rich stores of gold and silver in South America. The Asante (Ghana) system of evaluating gold dust by weight was familiar to African and European traders. Some of these brass weights had the form of tiny representations of people going about their daily lives, while others portrayed familiar scenes and objects or had geometric patterns.

Spain had a silver coin worth eight *reales*. These coins were often called "pieces of eight." Because the silver was soft, the coin could be cut into pieces to serve the need for smaller denominations. A fourth of the coin earned the name "two bits," a term that is still used for a quarter of a United States dollar.

About 1,200 years ago the Chinese produced the first paper money. Two centuries later the Chinese government established a bank to print and issue paper money. Today we are accustomed to ordering by telephone or electronic mail and to paying by check or credit card, as well as by coins and paper currency.

Discussion and Activities

Discussion

Initiate a discussion about recent experiences with the use of money. (Many children today have little opportunity to make independent purchases—in many areas the neighborhood candy store or grocery store is a thing of the past or never existed.) Did students have the exact amount required or did they receive change of a larger amount? How did numbers enter into the transaction? Were numbers spoken or written, and was computation necessary? If your childhood experience was different from your students', share your recollections with them. They might ask older family members about their childhood experiences with money.

Role play

Students might pretend that they live in a culture that uses cowrie shells or beads as currency. Children might actually string beads, buttons, macaroni shells, or other suitable objects on cord or pipe cleaners and make tables to show the relationships of the various units described in the text. Another set of relationships describes the use of beads as currency in the Congo (Zaire) region:

> 5 beads = a string
> 5 strings = 25 beads = *matanu* (a "five")
> 2 *matanu* = 50 beads = *lufuku*

Which U.S. coins correspond to these denominations?

Groups of students might set up a market situation, assign prices to their products, and carry out transactions with bead or shell money. They should be encouraged to use mental arithmetic. People who traded with beads or shells generally did not use pencil and paper! If nonliterate market women and men could compute mentally, our students can also learn to do so. For example, compute mentally the number of beads in 3 lufuku, 1 matanu, 2 strings, and 4 beads. [Answer: 189 beads.]

Research
Encourage students to research the use as currency of objects that had intrinsic value, such as beads, shells, and metal objects. Each group of students might undertake a different aspect and make a poster to illustrate the results of their research. It would be valuable to compare each type with the paper money and coinage we use today.

Print paper money
Students might print their own paper money in imitation of the Chinese of several hundred years ago, and carry out transactions with the use of the *suan pan*, the Chinese abacus (see page 99).

Research
Encourage students to research various forms of money in history and in different parts of the world. The foreign exchange columns of the daily newspaper list the currencies of many countries. Why does each country have a different form of currency? Does the value remain the same over a period of weeks or months?

Discuss earning money

It may be appropriate for your class to discuss the question of earning money. Perhaps they themselves earn money for services like baby-sitting, or they might discuss the allowances they receive. Relate the money received to the time factor: so much per hour or the amount earned within a month or a year. Students might role-play discussions with a parent or other family member about the size of an allowance, each side preparing arguments, backed up by specific figures, for how the money is to be used. Older students might role-play the negotiations between a group of workers in a union and their employers' committee.

KEEPING TRACK OF TIME

Background

When did humans start to keep track of time? Some say that women initiated the recording of time to keep track of their monthly cycles. Certainly the engraved marks on the Ishango bone (see page 92) seem to coincide with the cycles of the moon. The first calendars were probably lunar; solar calendars came later, when agriculturalists needed to know the time of year for planting the seed and the coming of the rains. Eventually society had to reconcile the two types of calendars. Astronomy and mathematics developed hand in hand.

In ancient Egypt the land had to be redivided each year after the flooding of the Nile River, the lifeline of the region. It seems likely that the Egyptian calendar goes back to about 4241 B.C.E. Each year began with the day on which the star Sirius rose in the same place as the sun, about the time that the Nile reached flood stage. The calendar was divided into three seasons—floodtime, seedtime, and harvest time—and each season consisted of four thirty-day months. Five festival days brought the total to 365, and adjustments were made from time to time for the extra quarter-day in the solar year. The Egyptian solar calendar was more accurate than many later efforts.

Mesopotamia, with its well-developed agriculture, devised an interesting calendar many thousands of years ago. Observing that the lunar cycle was twenty-nine and a half days, the Mesopotamians adjusted the number of days in their months so that they alternated between thirty and twenty-nine, giving a total of 354 days in a year. To make up for the annual difference between 354 and 365¼, they added an extra month to a year seven times in the course of nineteen calendar years, and occasionally adjusted the length of the month. For the most part the Jewish calendar follows this pattern; time is reckoned from our year 3761 B.C.E. as the starting point.

Both the Chinese and the Islamic calendars are lunar. Islamic months also alternate between thirty and twenty-nine days to give a total of 354 days, and reckoning began with the year that we call 622 C.E.

The Maya were great astronomers. Not only did they maintain a calendar based on a 365-day year for everyday use, but they also had a 260-day calendar for ritual purposes. Both were based on twenty-day "months." Thirteen such periods made up the ritual calendar, while the everyday calendar had eighteen twenty-day months plus five additional days.

People also had to keep track of time from one day to the next. The sun was usually their guide, and they named the periods of the day after the activities that took place—"time to fetch water," "time to milk the cows." By observing the apparent movements of the stars at night and the sun during the day, the Egyptians originated the division of the day into twenty-four equal hours. As life became more complex, clocks were invented. The sundial is the oldest method of telling time. A dial casts a shadow on a circular face subdivided into hours or periods, and the shadow points to the time. Egyptian sundials go back about three thousand years. (At night, the moon and stars were the guide.)

A later invention was the water clock, called a *clepsydra*. It was adjusted so that water flowed from one vessel to another at a fixed rate. Marks on the vessel showed how much time had elapsed. In the year 1086 the Chinese built a water clock that filled a forty-foot tower. Muslim scientists adapted the water clock to their needs—to tell the time for prayers, for example. Several centuries later Europeans invented and improved the mechanical clock.

So far we have discussed divisions of time based on natural phenomena—the cycles of the moon and the sun and the rotation of the earth. But human activities also created the need for divisions of time. We have a seven-day week, but the number seven is not universal. In many areas markets are held at regular intervals called "weeks," four or eight days in some parts of Nigeria, five days in other parts.

Discussion and Activities

Class discussion of time

Discuss the importance of time. What are some of the ways that we measure time? Why don't we measure time by our activities, as some societies do: the time to get up, the time to go to school, and so forth?

Class discussion of our calendar

Make sure that students understand our calendar—the number of days in a year, the varying number of days in our months, the fact that we also subdivide into seven-day weeks. They should distinguish between the divisions that depend upon natural phenomena and those that are arbitrary.

Research on origins

It's interesting to trace the origin of some subdivisions. Did the Maya use a twenty-day "month" because their numeration system groups by twenties? How does our subdivision of an hour into sixty minutes relate to the Mesopotamian base-sixty numeration system?

Research on names

Why is the ninth month in our calendar called September, which means seventh? The names of October, November, and December come from the Roman (Latin) words for eight, nine, and ten, respectively. Find out why! What other English words are based on these Latin number names? Can students name the months in other languages? Perhaps parents can help.

Research and comparisons

Each group might research a calendar that is different from ours, and compare it with ours in as many ways as possible. They can make posters to list their conclusions, and illustrate them with a one-year time line.

Research on dates for holidays

How do we set the dates for holidays like New Year's Day and Labor Day? Students might investigate how dates for sacred days are set in various religions. Family and community members may be knowledgeable about such matters. For example, why does the Muslim holy month of Ramadan rotate through the year? How about the varying dates for Easter and Passover? Check several calendars—the Muslim and Jewish calendars, for example—for the dates on which they celebrated New Year's Day this year or last year.

Mathematics of Maya calendars

Challenge upper-grade students to calculate the interval in days between two successive New Year's Days that coincide in both Maya calendars— the 365-day everyday calendar and the 260-day ritual calendar. What is the greatest common divisor (GCD) of both numbers? What is the lowest common multiple (LCM)? [GCD is 5; LCM is 18,980; 18,980 days, or fifty-two 365-day years; $5 \times 18,980 = 260 \times 365 = 94,900$]

Working with time zones

A discussion of the twenty-four time zones around the world can be tied in with the study of various cultures. How many hours would it take to fly to some of these zones? Take into account the north-south distances (latitudes), as well as the east-west distances (longitudes).

Inventing a calendar

Suggest that students try to improve upon our calendar by inventing one of their own. Which features of the calendar would they change? Which would they retain?

MEASURING AND ESTIMATING

Background

> The old system of weights and measures in our country is irregular, difficult to learn, and inconvenient to apply. . . . Originating by chance, rather than by science, [these measures] lacked the simplicity of law; and were, therefore, irregular and chaotic. . . . [The metric] system will, without doubt, in a few years be in general use in our country.

Although these words may seem contemporary, they were written by Dr. Edward Brooks in *The Normal Union Arithmetic*, published in Philadelphia in 1877.

As I write, the United States is still using that "irregular and chaotic" system decried by Dr. Brooks over a century ago, the only major country that has not yet gone completely metric. "U.S. Moving, Inch by 25.4 mm, to Metric System" was the heading in the *World Almanac's* section on the metric system.

When I visited Nigeria in the summer of 1974, that country had just made three major changes official: from the old British currency system to one based on the decimal system, from the British customary system of measures to the metric system, and from driving on the left side of the road to driving on the right. All of those new ways of thinking in just a few months! Of course, many people still used the old words; a market woman might quote a price of ten *naira* (the new Nigerian unit) as "ten shillings," but she really was referring to the price in nairas.

When people lived in small communities and exchanged goods by barter, they had little need for accurate measurements. Measures of length were often based on parts of the body. In fact, the "foot" is still part of our system of measurement. Other measures were the palm, the handspan, and the cubit. The cubit was the measure of the distance from the elbow to the tip of the middle finger. A long distance might be described as a "journey of four days."

Of course, a measure that is based on parts of the body is, at best, only approximate. Whose body are we to measure? If you were planning to buy five cubits of cloth, you might want to bring along a neighbor with the longest arm, while the merchant would prefer a short-armed person. Standardization became a necessity. Eventually government organizations established systems of standard units. The British Magna

■ **FIGURE 7–2 Measuring units based on parts of the body**

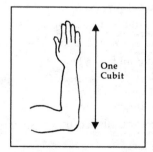 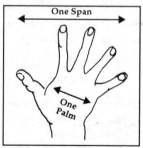 

∎ FIGURE 7–3 Yup'ik elder Joshua Phillip used the width of his fingers to measure the openings for the fishtrap he made. Note the computer in the background. Photograph by Claudia Zaslavsky

Carta spelled out weights and measures for certain items, and later other standards were imposed. In the time of Leonardo da Vinci, each city in Italy had its standard *braccia* (arm length), but it varied from Florence to Rome to Milan.

The existence of standard measures does not mean that people have given up on informal measures in favor of the standards. In spite of the fact that my parents owned a store in which they sold material by the yard, measuring with a yard-long metal rod attached to the edge of the counter, my mother would approximate a yard for her own purposes by stretching the material along her extended arm to the tip of her nose. I am sure she was not aware of the fact that the yard was standardized as the distance from the nose to the tip of the middle finger of the outstretched arm of a British king.

About 4,600 years ago the ancient Egyptians undertook the construction of the Great Pyramid of the Pharaoh Khufu, one of the Seven Wonders of the World. To this day scientists are amazed by the accuracy of measurement in its construction and alignment, an impossibility without standardized units of measure. The *royal cubit*, the measure used in construction, was about fifty-two centimeters in length. It was subdivided into seven *palms*, each again subdivided into four *digits*, or finger-widths. A shorter cubit was also in use. Other measures were the *hayt* (one hundred cubits) and the *double remen* (the length of the diagonal of a square whose side measured one royal cubit).

We can trace our units of measure to the Romans of two thousand years ago. Like the Egyptians, they were great builders and needed a standardized system. The word for *foot* in Latin is *pes*, from which we derive words like *pedestal* and *pedal*.

For the seafaring Vikings, the depth of the ocean water was crucial. A Viking seaman would lower a rope with a lead weight attached to the end. When it hit bottom, he would pull it up, measuring the length of the rope against his outstretched arms. This measure came to be called a "fathom," and later was standardized at six feet (about 1.8 meters).

When Spaniards invaded the land now known as Mexico, they found large cities and impressive buildings. Aztec measures of land were actually more accurate than those of the Spanish. They had a standard unit of area called a square *quahuitl*, in contrast to the Spanish *caballería*, which varied from farm to farm. The Aztec had measuring ropes marked off in *quahuitls* (each about 2.5 meters in length) and fractions of the unit. Because the size and the value of each piece of land was recorded and formed the basis for taxation, measurements were made carefully. This was frequently a difficult task, due to the mountainous terrain and the irregular shapes of the farms.

The history of the development of systems of weight and measures is a fascinating subject, intimately tied in with the economic life of a society. We now have instruments for making extremely accurate measurements, yet we must always remember that no measurement is ever exact.

Discussion and Activities

Discussion of informal methods of measurement
Ask students to demonstrate their informal methods of showing length. Do they hold their fingers or hands apart to show a certain distance? How do they deal with weight?

Discussion of body measures
It's a valuable experience for students to relate various standard units of measure to parts of their own bodies, to give them a feel for these measures. Perhaps a centimeter is the width of a fingernail, and so on.

Estimation
Working with partners, students might estimate a certain length—ten centimeters, for example—by holding their hands the appropriate distance apart. The estimates should be written down. Then the partners measure to see how accurately they have estimated. Some students are so fearful of being wrong that they are reluctant to estimate. This activity might help them to overcome their fears.

Research on nonstandard measures
Have students ask their family members and other adults about informal measures they learned when they were younger.

Measuring in personal feet
Working with partners, have students trace their feet on stiff paper and cut out the outline to form a personal "foot" measure. Partners measure each other's heights in personal feet and fractions of a foot. Record the height of each student in terms of that student's foot measure. An adult's height is about six or seven times the length of the foot. It would be interesting to discover whether this ratio holds true for younger people.

Food measures
Cooking and serving food are excellent activities to provide practice with estimation and units of measure and weight. Measures might be given as a teaspoonful or a cup. Are these standard or informal (nonstandard) measures? How can recipes be adjusted to feed more or fewer people?

■ FIGURE 7–4 Clara estimates how far to roll dough. Photograph by Sam Zaslavsky

Suppose a recipe for two people calls for one egg; what quantity of egg should be used if the dish is to serve only one person? Can a baker estimate how far to roll the dough to fit a nine-inch pie pan?

Older people often remember quantities in recipes as a pinch of this and a handful of that. Perhaps students can collect and record such recipes.

Why standardize? Role play

Discuss with students the advantages and disadvantages of informal measures such as those based on parts of the body. Each group might present a skit demonstrating what happens when nonstandard units are used in situations requiring standardization. An example is the story of the queen's bed, as told in Rolf Myller's *How Big Is a Foot?* (1991). The king orders a bed for the queen, giving the measurements in terms of the length of his own foot. The carpenter, however, uses his little apprentice's foot as the unit. Imagine the disastrous outcome!

Research
Have the students research the history of the development of systems of measurement in various societies and periods in history. What was the influence on the units we use today? Each group of students might undertake a different culture and make an illustrated poster or write a report that can be incorporated into a class book.

Metric prefixes
Ask students to compare the metric system with the customary (foot-pound) system of weights and measures. Are students familiar with the prefixes used in the metric system? Which system requires a greater use of calculations? Which system is easier to memorize?

Students should become familiar with the most common prefixes used in the metric system. The words denoting a multiple of a unit are derived from Greek, while those denoting a fractional part of a unit are from Latin. The following words refer to the meter, a unit of length, but are applicable to other units as well:

From Greek:
*Deka*meter = 10 meters
*Hecto*meter = 100 meters
*Kilo*meter = 1,000 meters

From Latin:
*Deci*meter = 0.1 meter (1/10 meter)
*Centi*meter = 0.01 meter (1/100 meter)
*Milli*meter = 0.001 meter (1/1,000 meter)

Research and discussion: Why are we behind the times?
Discuss with students the fact that the United States is the only major country that has not converted completely to metric. What factors have held us back? To what extent have weights and measures been metricized in our country?

Measure the earth
Advanced students will be fascinated to learn how Eratosthenes, a scholar at the university in Alexandria, Egypt, estimated the

circumference of the earth over 2,200 years ago using shadows, angles, and proportions. Most histories of mathematics include the story.

DATA COLLECTION

Background

How would our society function if it did not have efficient methods of collecting data? Not only does our government carry out a national census every ten years in which it tries to count every person, but it also issues annual updates based on samples of the total population. School administrators must know how many classrooms are required and how many books to order. Manufacturing plants and retail establishments keep track of inventory, requirements for various materials, and sales. Environmental groups and other advocacy organizations present data to back up their arguments. The list is endless!

Chapter 10 offers suggestions for specific activities involving the collection of data in the students' own communities. The discussion here is more general.

Discussion and Activities

Discussion

Ask students to discuss their experiences with data collection. Have they ever kept score in a game? Counted guests to invite to a party? Perhaps they counted their T-shirts and decided that they must buy new ones. Have students discuss data collection with family members to learn their experiences and report to the class.

Why collect data?

Why is data collection necessary for the running of our society? In what types of society and under what conditions is or was data collection of less importance?

Presenting data

In what forms are data presented? Ask students to bring in examples of written texts, tables, charts, graphs, and any other forms. Show them on the overhead projector and discuss sources, arrangement of numbers, and ease or difficulty in reading and interpreting the numbers.

Conduct a class census

Discuss with students the possibility of a class census. What questions should be in the questionnaire? How will they conduct the census? How will they display the data? Can they use the data for some important purposes?

Discussion of careers

Students may be interested in the types of careers that involve the collection of data. Does a teacher have to collect data? Students may be surprised to learn the importance of data collection in many fields. This is the "information age"!

Chapter 8

Geometry & Measurement in Architecture

Mathematical Topics
Geometry of shapes, measurement in one, two, and three dimensions, computation, scale drawing, ratios, patterns, logical thinking.

Cultural Connections
Africa: Ancient Egypt, Kenya, Tanzania, Cameroon, Nigeria, Zimbabwe; Central Asia; Europe: Ancient Greece and Rome; North America: Inuit (northern Canada), Iroquois, Plains Indian, Southwest United States (Pueblo, Anasazi).

Linked Subject
Architecture

THE ARCHITECTURE OF PEOPLE'S HOMES

Background

I like to start a discussion on people's homes by asking the participants to think about a possible design for a small summer house, nothing elaborate. Then I ask them to sketch the floor plan for this house. In most cases the floor plan is in the shape of a rectangle, or several combined rectangles. We are accustomed to a culture of straight lines and right angles. Imagine placing our rectangular sofas and beds and tables in round rooms!

But there are other ways to build. The words of the Oglala Lakota (Sioux) leader Black Elk, retold in *Black Elk Speaks* (Neihardt 1961), are often quoted to indicate the contrasts in points of view. When his people were moved to barren reservations, he said: "We made these little gray houses of logs that you see, and they are square. It is a bad way to live, for there can be no power in a square. You have noticed that everything an Indian does is in a circle, and that is because the Power of the World always works in circles and everything tries to be round" (198). Black Elk's traditional home was a round tipi that women stitched together from buffalo hides. During the frequent moves to follow the buffalo, the tipis were dismantled and transported to the new campsites. The tipi was admirably suited to life on the Great Plains.

Does the round house possess any advantages over the rectangular shape to which we are accustomed? For one thing, it is easier to build. A round house may be supported chiefly by a center pole, while a rectangular structure requires supports at the four corners. For societies in which people build their own homes, without the aid of professional architects and construction workers, simple construction is an important consideration.

There is another consideration. When people have to gather or process the building materials themselves, often under conditions of great hardship, they want to build a home that offers the greatest possible amount of floor space for a given amount of material for the walls. The circular floor is the answer.

When I visited a *shamba* (farm) in Kenya belonging to the family of my son's student, this young man pointed to a round structure in the distance, situated in the midst of several larger rectangular buildings. "That is the old kind of Kamba house. Now they use it only for storage." His own family lived in a well-built rectangular house of sun-dried adobe bricks that he and his brother had molded themselves.

We are so accustomed to changes in our lives that we would probably adapt easily to living in rooms with novel shapes. For older people accustomed to a certain traditional way of life, change can be traumatic. In *Africa Counts* (Zaslavsky 1979, 163) I tell the story of Rodah's grandmother. Rodah and her husband had acquired six acres of land in the region of Kenya inhabited by the Kamba people. They had built several rectangular adobe structures—one for sleeping, one for eating, another for cooking, as was the custom. Proud of her new

■ FIGURE 8–1 Tipi of the Plains Indians

shamba, Rodah invited her grandparents to visit. "Do you live in a house with corners?" asked her grandmother. Told that they did, the grandmother replied, "No, we can't live in a house with corners. There is no pole to support the house. And besides, we would get lost in such a house!"

The traditional house of the Kamba people is constructed on a framework of young trees pushed into the ground in a circular arrangement and tied at the top to a thick post. Then a framework of parallel concentric circles is placed upon this foundation, and the whole structure is thatched with grasses.

■ FIGURE 8–2 Author in front of a round house, Tanzania. Photograph by Sam Zaslavsky

In recent years the round house has given way to rectangular structures in some parts of Africa. In the recently resettled lands of East Africa, where people like Rodah and her husband replaced the white settlers after Kenya had gained independence, the rectangular house with a metal roof is a common sight, as well as a symbol of higher status.

Many African people have been building rectangular houses for centuries, as I discovered when I visited the Village Museum on the outskirts of Dar es Salaam (Tanzania). Exhibited on this site were full-scale models of the many styles of houses commonly found in Tanzania. There were flimsy round thatched structures of nomadic cattle herders and sturdy six-room round houses of settled agriculturalists. Coastal people tended to live in rectangular homes, perhaps as a result of Muslim influence. In the hot inland region the Hehe people constructed the oblong *tembe*, many rooms surrounding an inner courtyard, with walls almost a foot thick—no need for air-conditioning.

The round house can take many forms—the small, roughly hemispheric structure, the beehive form of the Chagga on Mount

Kilimanjaro, the popular cone-cylinder style of the Kikuyu and of many other peoples. Occasionally one might see a rectangular house amidst a compound of round buildings, often an indication of the high status of the occupant, perhaps a son who has become a teacher or an official. In her charming storybook *The Village of Round and Square Houses* (1986), Ann Grifalconi suggests that a tradition about male and female roles is the reason for the presence of both round and square houses in the same village in Cameroon.

In the forest regions of Africa the rectangular house is the norm, often decorated with murals or sculptured clay. The Yoruba of southwest Nigeria and Benin have long lived in compounds of rectangular buildings constructed around an inner courtyard. Comparisons with ancient Roman and Egyptian architecture reveal similarities in style. Other similarities between Yoruba and Egyptian culture, language, and religion suggest the possibility that the people inhabiting these areas came originally from the Nile valley.

A few words about sensitivity to cultures are in order. In writing about Africa, the derogatory word *hut* is often used to describe the homes of African peoples. A similar structure in Europe or the United States might be called a *cottage* or a *cabin* or just a *house*. The implication is that Africans are too "primitive" to know how to build *real* houses.

What are some of the factors that influence the shape of a house? David Whitin posed this question to a class of fifth graders and described their responses in his book with Sandra Wilde, *Read Any Good Math Lately?* (1992). Below, I list their main categories and apply them to several cultures.

- The size of the family. Africans living in a round house might construct an additional building to accommodate a larger family; a rectangular home might have a room added.

- Environment. The kind of materials that are available influences the shape of the house. One cannot build a log cabin without logs, or a thatched cottage without thatch. The Haudenosaunee (Iroquois) longhouse would be impossible in an area devoid of trees.

- Climate. People want to stay cool in hot weather and warm in cold weather. The Inuit igloo, a round house, is quite

■ FIGURE 8–3 Yasmin's Iroquois longhouse of Popsicle sticks. Photograph by Sam Zaslavsky

comfortable in winter. Today the Inuit are more likely to live in homes that are similar to those in the United States. The Pueblo (Southwest United States) adobe houses are well suited to keep the occupants cool in the hot summers of the region.

• Terrain. Building on a hillside or mountaintop is quite different from building on a flat plain. In many regions of Africa, hillside structures are usually round and tall, involve the use of stone at least to some extent, and have decorated doorways, floors, and benches.

• Culture. The words of Black Elk illustrate the importance of the circle in his culture. In a recent conversation several African college mathematics instructors told me that their people held similar beliefs about the significance of the circle in their lives.

• Psychological factors. This may include the desire to be different, to be "modern," to reject traditions, or to conform to a local pattern.

• Historical traditions. Rodah's grandmother had lived all her life in a round house with a center pole. She could not imagine living in a different structure.

• Lifestyle. The tipi of the buffalo hunters of the Great Plains and the round yurt of the Central Asian herders are well suited to the nomadic way of life. Farmers construct houses that they expect will last a long time.

• An additional factor is whether the homes are constructed by professional builders or by the people who are going to live in them.

Discussion and Activities

Observe shapes

Start off by having students describe the shape of the classroom and of the rooms in their homes, paying particular attention to the shape of the floors, walls, ceilings, window and door frames, and other notable features. As students develop their powers of observation and attention to geometry in the environment, they will become aware of the predominance of straight lines and right angles (corners) in our culture. Can they find exceptions?

Discussion of size and shape

Have students discuss the types of dwellings with which they are familiar—single-family home, apartment house, tent, and so forth, with special attention to size and shape. Why do people choose one type rather than another? Ask students to observe the types of buildings in their neighborhood. Are buildings constructed differently for different purposes?

Younger children might read and discuss *The Village of Round and Square Houses* (Grifalconi 1986) or examine and discuss the photographs in *Houses and Homes* (Morris 1992). Older students might read the text and discuss the photographs in books like *Africa Counts* (Zaslavsky 1979) and *African Traditional Architecture* (Denyer 1978). Can they imagine the techniques involved in the construction of round versus square (or rectangular) houses? How does the builder determine the circumference of a circle? How does the builder know that a four-sided shape is really a rectangle or a square?

Discuss influences

What factors influence the way people build their homes? Can students give examples for each factor?

Design your own

Suggest that students design and draw a floor plan for a small summer house, described at the beginning of this chapter.

Experiment with area and perimeter

Students may perform the following experiment. Each person will need a sheet of grid paper and a piece of string thirty-two grid units in length. For centimeter-squared paper, the string should be thirty-two centimeters long. (If appropriate, young children may work with square floor tiles and a rope.)

> Imagine that you live in a society in which people must
> produce almost everything they need by their own efforts.
> Your family is planning to build a house. You and your family
> must gather all the materials, perhaps with the help of your
> neighbors. Some of the materials may be hard to come by, and
> you want to use as little as possible.
>
> Pretend that you have collected a certain amount of material
> for the walls (length of the string). Now you want to find out
> what shape will yield the largest floor space with this quantity
> of material. (Zaslavsky 1989, 20)

In mathematical terms, students are to determine the shape that has the largest *area* for a given *perimeter*.

Students work in pairs, but each student should draw at least the following figures, using the string to form a perimeter of thirty-two units: a circle, a square, a rectangle that is not square, a triangle, and possibly an irregular figure. They count the number of square grid units contained within each shape and arrange the data in a table.

Students may raise the following questions as they carry out this experiment. Encourage them to find solutions, possibly different from my suggestions.

- "How can we draw a good circle without using a compass?" (Work in pairs. One person holds the string while the other marks a few strategic points on the circumference. Then draw the circle freehand.)

- "How do we count fractions of grid squares?" (Remind them that all measurements are approximate; they should therefore decide the most feasible method of dealing with this question.

Some students may want to carry out the painstaking task of adding small fractions. Others will feel comfortable with counting as whole squares the fractions that seem larger than half, and ignoring those less than half.)

• "Counting all these little squares is so boring!" (Encourage them to look for symmetry. For example, divide the figure into congruent quarters, count the squares in one quadrant, and multiply by four.)

Students should discover that, with a given fixed perimeter:

1. The circle has the greatest area of any shape.
2. Of all rectangles, the square has the greatest area.
3. The larger the difference between the length and width of a rectangle, the smaller the area.
4. The formula for the area of a rectangle (but not of the other figures) is length times width.
5. A triangle has a smaller area than a square.
6. We use linear units to measure length and square units to measure area.

Were these conclusions different from those they expected? Can they draw any other conclusions from this experiment?

Older students might discuss the reasons for using a string thirty-two units long. Why not some other length? I have at least two good reasons for selecting this number: (1) thirty-two is divisible by four and is the perimeter of a square enclosing a whole number of grid squares; (2) a circle with a circumference of thirty-two units has a diameter of approximately ten units, a convenient number to work with. A smaller convenient number for the length of the string is sixteen.

Construct model houses
Students might construct models of the houses that are typical of one or more societies they are studying and write about them. This project can involve drawing to scale, calculating volume and surface area, analyzing cross sections and shadows, and sketching three-dimensional objects.

Draw floor plans
Students may enjoy drawing floor plans to scale of their own homes, showing the dimensions and area of rooms, hallways, closets (depending on their mathematical maturity).

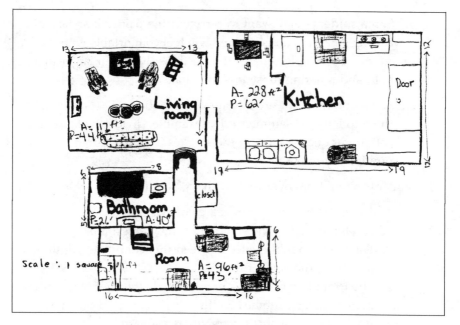

▮ **FIGURE 8–4 Floor plan of Eileen's apartment**

Observe repeated patterns
Look for repeated patterns in buildings—brickwork, window placement, decorative themes—and describe them in words and drawings.

Computer
Many of the activities described here can be adapted to the computer.

Discussion: Why straight walls?
Students may now be convinced that the circular house has the largest floor space for a given amount of materials for the walls. Why, then, are most of our buildings and rooms constructed with straight walls and right angles?

Discuss homelessness
As students reflect and talk about people's homes, they may be struck by the fact that some people are homeless. Encourage them to research and discuss the reasons for homelessness. What is the effect of homelessness on children? What do they think our society can do to overcome this problem?

OUTSTANDING BUILDINGS

Background

Once a society has attained a certain degree of wealth and power, it often celebrates this achievement by constructing spectacular buildings. The power may be that of secular or religious institutions or a combination of both. Some of these edifices have withstood the ravages of time for thousands of years.

Almost five thousand years ago the Egyptian pharaohs began to construct enormous stone pyramids, a memorial to the wealth and power of the divine kings and a tribute to the architects and craftsmen of the period. The age of the pyramids was short; in fact, the five largest pyramids were built within one century in the early period of Egyptian glory. Subsequently they erected impressive columned temples, as did the Mesopotamians and, later, the Greeks. Also in Africa is the city-state Great Zimbabwe ("great stone house") with its complex stone architecture and elliptical surrounding wall. Centuries ago it served as the seat of government for the rulers of a vast kingdom in southern Africa, and it now lends its name to the country called Zimbabwe.

In Europe, kings and nobles built palaces and fortified castles, and churches with tall spires and vaulted ceilings celebrated the power of the organized church. The temples and pagodas of East Asia, the Great Wall of China, the mosques of Islam with their intricate geometric decorations, the pyramids of the Maya—all these buildings still inspire awe in the viewer. Over two thousand years ago the inhabitants of Teotihuacán, near the present site of Mexico City, began the construction of a carefully planned city with about two thousand interlinked apartment complexes. Scientists estimate that about the year 600 c.e. it had 125,000 inhabitants. And a thousand years ago the Anasazi, ancestors of the Pueblo Indians of the Southwest, constructed Pueblo Bonito in Chaco Canyon, an apartment complex reaching five stories high and housing a thousand people. America would not see a taller apartment house until the nineteenth century.

Before constructing models of Egyptian pyramids for their mathematics class, eighth graders Marina Frants and Svetlana Fisher did extensive research, using *Science in Ancient Egypt* (Woods 1988) and other resources. After reading their reports and viewing their finished work, I asked them to write about the problems they had in carrying out the construction. Both girls were recent émigrés from the former Soviet Union. (I have made minor corrections in grammar and spelling. The Russian language does not use articles before nouns.)

Svetlana wrote:

> I had a problem with material of the pyramid. I needed to find a cardboard and thick paper for it. I didn't have many problems with building of pyramid except inside of the pyramid and the pier with corridor, because of the small things that I had to cut.

Indeed, the inside of her model is a marvelous construction, following closely the design of the Great Pyramid of the Pharaoh Khufu.

Marina used corrugated board for her model. Her initial problem was conceptual. She wrote:

> I had a few problems in making pyramid. First of all I didn't really know that in Egypt pyramids had square bases, so I built

■ FIGURE 8–5 Interior view of Svetlana's pyramid. Photograph by Sam Zaslavsky

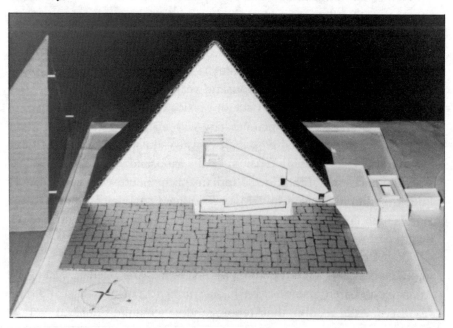

a triangular base pyramid, but I couldn't find any information about it. I started to change it to square base pyramid.

1. I cut the pyramid on the side and opened it.
2. Made another triangle and glued four of them together.
3. Glued the pyramid to the *square* base.

I also had a difficult time putting a triangular wall inside the pyramid. This wall doesn't stand straight, it lies down on about 15° on the base, but the top had to touch the vertex of the pyramid, and all four sides have to meet at the vertex too, otherwise you can't build a pyramid.

I did not have the opportunity to question Marina about the inner wall that "lies down on about 15° on the base," which I don't quite understand. Perhaps she meant 75°, but used the complement of the angle.

Discussion and Activities

Observe shapes of historical buildings

Show students photographs—or ask them to bring in photographs—of outstanding buildings of the past. Can they describe the features that identify the buildings as characteristic of certain societies or periods in history? They might look at the graceful curved roofs of Chinese temples or the tall spires of Gothic cathedrals. Are any of these structures round or elliptical (oval)? Two examples of such buildings are the Roman Colosseum and Great Zimbabwe. Show children the illustrations, based on the ruins of Great Zimbabwe, in John Steptoe's Caldecott Honor Book *Mufaro's Beautiful Daughters, An African Tale* (1987). Compare the Roman Colosseum to the elliptical or round stadiums we have today. Why are they constructed in that shape? Discuss the reasons for round towers on rectangular castles.

Construct scale models

Students might do research on specific buildings, write about them, and construct scale models.

Building the pyramids

Discuss the difficulties involved in the building of the pyramids. Scholars have not yet determined how the Egyptians were able to transport the tremendous building blocks to the heights required by the pyramids (481 feet for the Great Pyramid) and to lay them with such amazing accuracy. A 1992 Public Broadcasting System (PBS) program, *This Old Pyramid*, depicts a contemporary effort, not quite successful, to construct a small pyramid using ancient Egyptian technology.

Research shapes of contemporary buildings

Ask students to do research on outstanding buildings of the present era. I like to show photographs of skyscrapers in Hong Kong, New York, and Moscow, and ask my audience to guess where they are located. Some styles have become universal. On the other hand, the thirty-two-story Kenya International Conference Centre in Nairobi has as its base a many-sided polygon, almost a circle. Next to it stands a round auditorium with a conical roof, similar in shape to many homes in Kenya.

∎ **FIGURE 8–6 Kenya International Conference Centre, Nairobi. Courtesy of Kenya Mission to the United Nations**

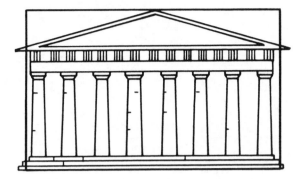

▮ **FIGURE 8–7 The Parthenon, Athens**

Research the golden ratio

One of the most beautiful buildings of ancient times was the Parthenon in ancient Greece. The ratio of the width to the height is called the golden ratio, approximately 1.6 to 1. A rectangle whose sides conform to the golden ratio is considered one of the most pleasing shapes. The golden ratio is common in nature and is also related to the Fibonacci number sequence, in which each number is the sum of the two preceding numbers—for example, 1, 1, 2, 3, 5, 8, 13, 21. . . . The ratio of each number to its predecessor is close to the golden ratio. Encourage interested students to research this topic and inform the class about their research.

Contact

The Salvadori Educational Center on the Built Environment offers literature and lesson plans: City College of New York, Harris Hall, Room 202, 138th Street and Convent Avenue, New York, NY 10031 (212) 650-5497.

Other activities

Review the suggestions in the earlier part of this chapter. Many are also applicable to the study of outstanding buildings.

 *Chapter 9*

Geometry, Measurement, & Symmetry in Art

Mathematical Topics
Geometry of shapes, measurement of angles and polygons, scale drawing, similarity, symmetry, repeated patterns, tessellations.

Cultural Connections
Africa: Ghana (Asante), Zaire (Kuba); Asia: China, Japan, Islam; North America: Yup'ik (southwest Alaska Eskimo), United States in general.

Linked Subject
Art: tangrams, paper folding, quilting, border patterns, block printing, tessellations.

In many societies art is widely diffused throughout the culture and the life of the individual. Art is not just something to hang on the wall or to display in a museum. Articles of everyday use, such as pottery, basketry, and textiles, are decorated in patterns that often have symbolic meaning. Indeed, archaeologists work hand in hand with mathematicians to identify ancient societies by analyzing patterns in decorated pottery and other surviving objects. A beautifully carved gameboard may be passed down from generation to generation. Art is also an integral part of the religious life of the community, as exemplified by masks, ceremonial dress, religious objects, and architectural elements.

Bringing math to life through the medium of art gives students the kinds of physical experiences that are essential for the development of spatial thinking. Geometric concepts have real meaning when they are presented in this concrete form. Art activities are open-ended; each student can take a project as far and in whatever direction he or she pleases. Beyond the mathematical benefits, art is a source of joy to young people. They can learn math, be creative, and have fun all at the same time.

Women have an important role in creating art. Sometimes the products of so-called women's work are assigned a low status by being referred to as crafts rather than art; this is true also of the works of non-Western societies. In her Maths in Work Project, British mathematician Mary Harris revealed the mathematics inherent in traditional women's work with textiles. One display in her traveling exhibit *Common Threads* compares the mathematical aspects of a design for a right-angled cylindrical pipe in a chemical factory with the mathematics of knitting the heel of a sock, and raises the question, Why is the industrial problem considered real mathematics, while the knitting problem is not taken seriously as valid mathematics?

Through art as the medium, the school can involve the families and communities of the students. Children may learn from their parents or grandparents some of the techniques that are getting lost in our machine-made culture. Invite local artists to visit the classroom and demonstrate their expertise. Families may want to exhibit art objects from other lands and the distant past.

Art is a rich field for the exploration of many concepts in geometry and measurement—size, shape, angle measurement, similarity, symmetry, and repeated patterns, including tessellations. Any of the activities suggested below involves more than one of these concepts. I will discuss several types of activities as examples of the possibilities in the mathematics-art connection. You may want to link such activities to lessons in art or to the societies discussed in social studies classes.

POLYGONS

Discussion and Activities

Observe the environment

Ask students to point out various polygons that they see in their environment and identify them by name, if possible. Which polygons are regular—all sides of equal length and all angles of equal measurement?

Tangrams

Tangrams originated in China and became popular in other parts of the world in the nineteenth century. Tangram pieces are seven polygons cut from a square so that the measures of their sides are in specific relationships.

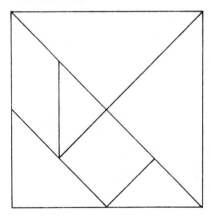

Shape, area, and perimeter. Challenge students to arrange the *tans* to form pleasing designs or to rearrange the pieces to form other polygons, including the original square. Do students understand that all the figures they create have the same area (provided they use all seven tans), no matter how the shape changes? They might also note that the perimeters vary while the area remains the same.

Young children will enjoy *Grandfather Tang's Story* (Tompert 1990), about two animals who escape being caught by transforming themselves into different shapes. Various combinations of tangrams illustrate the shapes of the animals.

PAPER FOLDING

Background

Who has not done paper folding and cutting to make Valentine hearts, Christmas trees, Thanksgiving pumpkins, and elaborate six-pointed snowflakes? Here we will discuss two types of Japanese paper-folding activities—*mon-kiri* and *origami*.

Discussion and Activities

Mon-Kiri

The practice of cutting designs in paper has a long history in both China and Japan and requires a great deal of skill. Samurai warriors decorated their armor with these designs. The simple design in this activity is similar to a snowflake, except that it will have four-fold rather than six-fold symmetry. Dr. Beverly Ferrucci, an instructor at Keene State College in New Hampshire, has her students follow this procedure:

1. Cut a six-inch circle of white paper. Fold it four times so that it has eight layers.

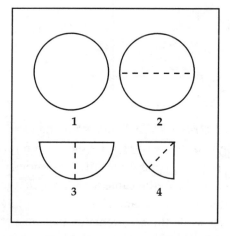

2. Draw and cut a design. All lines must touch the outer edges and no lines may touch.
3. Open the design and glue it onto a six-inch square of black paper. You may want to trim the black paper before gluing it onto a seven-inch red square. Glue the red paper to an eight-inch black square.

Beverly poses the following questions:

1. What types of angles do you see in each step of the design?
2. How many layers of paper do you have after making each fold?
3. How do changes in your original cuts affect your design when it is open?

Origami

Introduce this ancient Japanese art through the book *Sadako and the Thousand Cranes* (Coerr 1977), a true story about a victim of radiation poisoning as a result of the bombing of Hiroshima in World War II. The belief was that she would live if she and her friends folded a thousand cranes. Sadly, she died before achieving this goal. Specific instructions for making origami figures are available in *The ABCs of Origami* (Sarasas 1964) and other references.

QUILT DESIGNS

Background

As I walked through the lobby of a local elementary school, two beautiful hangings, truly works of art, caught my attention. One was a patchwork quilt top of thirty squares in a five-by-six array. Geometrically the squares were identical, based on the combination of small squares and right triangles that form the Ohio Star motif. For a varied and

∎ **FIGURES 9–1A & B Patchwork and appliqué hangings by students of P.S. 189, Manhattan. Photographs by Sam Zaslavsky**

pleasing effect, each square was composed of a different combination of patterned cloth, quite a feat for a fourth-grade class. The teacher explained that she had been an art major, the class was studying the colonial period, and she wanted them to get a feeling for life in those times. She spoke of art and social studies, but not of mathematics! When I asked whether the boys had objected to sewing, she said: "I told them that tailors sew. No problem whatsoever."

Next to the patchwork quilt was a fifth-grade art project consisting of sixteen felt squares to which had been sewed smaller felt squares of various sizes and colors. Each large square of the four-by-four array was unique. What an impressive way to use the square as a motif!

Quilting was introduced to the American colonies by settlers from England and the Netherlands and by Africans brought to the continent as slaves. For women who were restricted in their activities, the quilting bee provided an acceptable social gathering. Women would gather to make quilts for special occasions—a wedding of a son or daughter, the arrival of a new minister, the departure of a family for the West. Quilting was often a woman's sole means of artistic expression. One woman wrote: "It took me near twenty-five years to make that quilt. My whole life is in that quilt." Some African American women were able to purchase their freedom from slavery with their beautiful quilts, often based on African patterns.

Both the designs and the quilts have been handed down from generation to generation. Some examples became part of museum collections, a celebration of women's contributions to the arts over the years. Quilting is becoming ever more popular as a hobby, while professional artists are testing their designs on the computer before applying them to cloth.

In her inspiring book *Garbage Pizza, Patchwork Quilts, and Math Magic* (1993), Susan Ohanian tells of an eastern Kentucky school district that was looking for a way to involve parents in their children's math learning. Many of the parents had not finished high school, and the prospect of doing math was intimidating. A paper quilt project, introduced through the Parent Art Council, was the solution. As the school coordinator commented, "It is easier to recruit parents for an art project than for a math project. We designed art projects that would reinforce math concepts" (185). Many parents were already knowledgeable about quilts and were eager to become involved. Ohanian writes, "Parents who have always considered themselves 'bad at math' see that they had very definite skills to share with the children, skills of academic value" (186).

The square is the basic shape for the patchwork quilt. The designs may vary from one square to the other, or the entire quilt may be composed of squares having identical designs but varied colors or types of fabric, like the one the fourth graders displayed in the school lobby. Because the Shoo Fly and Ohio Star motifs are among the simplest, I use them as a basis for discussion, but there is no need to limit yourself to these patterns. Teachers are often amazed by the complexity of their students' creations.

 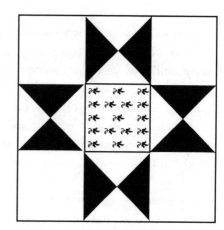

▪ FIGURE 9–2 Quilt blocks: Shoo Fly and Ohio Star

Discussion and Activities

Observe quilt patterns

Young children will enjoy reading a story about quilts and seeing the pictures. Adult books with illustrations of the great variety of quilt blocks and photographs of actual quilts are intriguing to all students. Ohanian's book includes illustrations of many simple quilt blocks and paper quilts made by primary school children.

Quilt display

Students or their parents may have treasured quilts to display to the class. Perhaps a local quilt maker can be persuaded to visit and discuss his or her work.

Mathematical analysis of a quilt block

Ask the students to choose one quilt block. Let's assume that they have chosen either the Shoo Fly or Ohio Star pattern. Give the students copies of the pattern and ask them to write about it. They may note any of the following features, depending on the mathematical topics they have studied:

1. *Shapes.* Name the geometric shapes. How many of each? What are their colors? Describe or draw diagrams to show how you can put together two or more shapes to make a different shape or a larger shape of the same kind.

2. *Measurement.* Describe the relationships among the lengths of the sides of the different shapes. State the angle measurements of each shape.

3. *Symmetry.* Students may have questions about the symmetry of the designs in handmade quilts. Accustomed to the near perfection of design in factory-made patterns, they may consider the flaws in handcrafted quilts to be violations of symmetry. Encourage them to consider the intentions of the artist and to overlook insignificant or unavoidable deviations from perfection, an ideal that can never be achieved in the real world. Some kinds of symmetry include:

a. *Line (or fold) symmetry.* Analyze the three-by-three square quilt block for line symmetry. Can you fold the block in half so that one half of the design matches the other half? An alternative is the mirror test. If you placed a mirror upright on the fold line, would the reflection in the mirror look the same as the half of the design behind the mirror? How many different fold lines are there? Make sketches, showing the fold lines as dotted lines. [Four: one horizontal, one vertical, and two diagonal. The square has *line symmetry of order four.*]

b. *Rotational symmetry.* Analyze the three-by-three square quilt block for turn symmetry. Rotate the block slowly until the design looks the same as it did in the original position. In how many different positions does the design look the same, including the original position? Through what angle does the block turn each time? [Four; 90°. The square has *rotational symmetry of order four.*] A helpful (but not always feasible) test for turn symmetry is to trace the design on a sheet of thin paper and label one corner of both squares. Place a pin, pencil point, or fingertip on the center of both squares. Then rotate one square slowly until the designs on the two squares match. Continue rotating until the free square is back in its original position.

c. *Color symmetry.* A design may have symmetry with respect to its shape but not its color. (To take an unlikely but easily explained example, suppose that the left half of the quilt block is done in shades of blue and the right half in shades of yellow.) Depending on students' age and mathematical background, encourage them to analyze both shape and color.

Sometimes a design is symmetrical except for one small element. Students should note such exceptions.

4. *Similarity*. Suppose you want to make a quilt block that has a side twice as long as the side of the model square. How many times as much paper or fabric will you need? Suppose it is three times as long? Can you make a general statement about similar squares? [Four; nine; if the quilt block is n times as long as the model, it will require n^2 as much material.]

Construct a quilt block

Have each student put together one three-by-three square quilt block of construction paper. Give each student nine identical squares of one color and nine of another color. They can cut some of the squares into triangles and put together quilt blocks of their own design.

Make a quilt

Encourage each group of students, or the class as a whole, to plan and construct a large quilt of construction paper, each student contributing one or more squares. Perhaps they are sufficiently ambitious to sew a fabric patchwork quilt top. They should start with a labeled scale drawing of the quilt block. Ask them to describe in writing, with illustrations, the reason they selected a particular design, how the design was constructed, colors they used, the geometric concepts, difficulties they encountered in carrying out the project, and how they felt about doing the project.

Computers

Students with some computer graphics experience and adequate facilities can design quilt squares on the computer. A good project would be for these students to write and illustrate a booklet about quilt design on the computer.

Exhibit

Arrange a quilt exhibit for the corridors of your school. Call in parents and the press to tell the community about it.

Extension to other shapes

Encourage students to analyze and write about symmetrical designs in various cultures, as they did with the quilt patterns. How is the design used, and what is its history and significance? The ankh, the peace symbol, the five- or six-pointed star, and the Chinese yin/yang all have distinctive geometric form and symmetry, as well as symbolic significance. The flags of many countries are a fruitful source of symbols.

REPEATED PATTERNS IN BORDERS

Yup'ik Border Patterns: Background

The Yup'ik (Eskimo) live along the southwestern coast of Alaska. The borders of Yup'ik parkas provide a fine example of traditional repeated patterns. During the first several weeks of school, Yup'ik teacher Esther Ilutsik spends a few minutes a week informally introducing her Yup'ik primary school students to the names and meaning of the different patterns. After her students have become familiar with the patterns, she has the children bring in (from home or from magazines) photos of parkas with border patterns. The children make photocopies of their pictures and combine them in a poster that identifies the appropriate name of each pattern; alternatively, they may draw their favorite patterns on a poster. As the children, working in pairs, learn to reproduce and color the patterns, Esther comments on their work and emphasizes the traditional Yup'ik pattern names, words meaning mountains, window, sled runners, and "put little things together." Drawing these patterns generates a great deal of enthusiasm, and all children eagerly join in the activity.

Esther continues: "The next few lessons are on reproducing patterns by name and having the children take a lead in this activity. For example, one child will ask the other children to create a 'braid' pattern. This child then checks work and the one who completes it first and correctly gets to be the next leader." She then combines two aspects of Yup'ik culture by having the children "try to put the patterns to drum beats. The other children try to find the correct pattern. The child then has to explain his 'rule.' "

■ FIGURE 9–3 Traditional Yup'ik border patterns

Finally, after these lively activities, Esther discusses the geometric terms for the patterns—square, triangle, diamond, and so on—as well as the appropriate vocabulary for the operations—translations (slides), rotations (turns), reflections (flips), and magnification (stretching or enlarging).

I was invited to Alaska to attend a conference arranged by University of Alaska instructors for teachers and teacher aides in predominantly Yup'ik schools, as well as Yup'ik elders, held at the end of the school year to plan curriculum for the following year. The topic under discussion one afternoon was patterns and symmetry. All the participants were women; the men were off in another room discussing the traditional Yup'ik calendar. Each person received an envelope of precut posterboard squares and isosceles right triangles, two sizes of each. After the participants had used the materials to form border patterns, Dr. Claudette Bradley, a University of Alaska instructor, reviewed the concepts of geometric transformations—symmetry, translation or slide, reflection, rotation, and magnification or stretching.

The next task was to assign proper Yup'ik terminology to each of these concepts, as bilingual teachers or aides translated for the elders who did not speak English. After much discussion in both Yup'ik and English, one of the teachers wrote the terms in both languages on the chalkboard. They translated *symmetry* into the Yup'ik words for *same measure*. Because of differences in the dialects of Yup'ik spoken in different regions of western Alaska, some terms were translated into two alternative forms. One translation of *reflection* meant *mirror*, while another borrowed from the terminology of sewing. A participant commented that in her region the vocabulary was slightly different and she would have to consult the elders when she went home.

One teacher displayed two parkas that her mother had made many years before. Both her mother and her aunt were among the elders at the conference, and you can imagine their pride in having this work used as a basis for mathematics lessons. Borders on parkas became the theme for the next activity. The participants worked in groups to design lessons based on the use of the manipulatives and the vocabulary of transformations. Each teacher or aide explained her lesson, both the mathematical and the cultural aspects, using the overhead projector to enlarge the patterns. Esther Ilutsik discussed the activities that she had already carried out the previous year, which I described above.

Kathryn Schubeck, Esther's fellow teacher at Aleknagik Elementary School, typed her lesson plan on the computer, drew the necessary illustrations based on the border of one of the models, and distributed copies to all the participants. In her lessons she covered not only the concepts that the group had discussed, but also area and the relationship among the three sides of a right triangle, all based on the repeating pattern in the parka border.

Before going on to patterns in dance fans, some of the participants

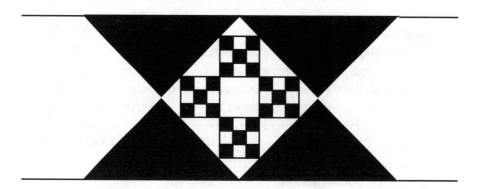

■ FIGURE 9–4 Traditional Yup'ik parka border pattern

played the following game. Two people sat back to back. One person made a pattern, which she described to her colleague in the Yup'ik language. That person then made the pattern based on her interpretation of the description. When they compared the outcomes, they analyzed their mistakes. Did they result from an insufficient or misleading description or from a failure to follow directions? Students will have a lot of fun playing that game.

Mathematical Analysis of Repeated Border Patterns

In a border pattern, a motif is repeated along one direction. The best way to analyze the mathematical operations is to start with a rectangular stencil into which a motif has been cut and a set of "tracks" along which the stencil will move. The operations are those we have already discussed—slide, half-turn, and flip, as the children like to say. In more mathematical language, we'll be working with operations called *translations* (slides), *rotations of 180°* (half-turns), and *reflections* in either a *horizontal* or *vertical axis* (flips). Another mathematical term is *glide reflection*, which consists of a horizontal flip and a slide in one operation. By repeating one operation or a combination of operations, we find that there are exactly seven different ways to repeat a pattern along one direction.

Start with a track of two parallel lines subdivided into rectangles to match the size and shape of the rectangular stencil. Then follow the directions for the first five types. The last two types require a double track to accommodate horizontal flips. The sequence of motions is indicated by arrows and by the numbers next to each rectangle. See pages 154 and 155.

Discussion and Activities

Border patterns with stamps

Stamps can be made from such materials as sponges, potato halves, and foam pads with self-adhesive backing so that they can be attached to blocks of wood. Suggest that students use their stamps to create borders for place mats, book covers, etc. First they should draw a track. They might slide the stamp from one position to the next (Type 1), or give it a half-turn every time the design is repeated (Type 2).

Border patterns with stencils

Students will find that they cannot use a stamp to produce reflections of the motif. They will need a different technique. One way is to cut out a design and trace it. An alternative is to make a stencil by cutting a design into a rectangle of heavy paper or plastic. The design should not have horizontal or vertical symmetry, because that might limit the variety of patterns. (Can students prove this statement?) Older students might study the seven types and select one or two types as a basis for their own creations.

Computers

Encourage students with access to computers and with the necessary know-how to develop a computer program that can generate repeated patterns for a border.

Observation in the environment

Once students have created their own repeated patterns, they will become aware of repeated patterns in their environment, in books and magazines. Encourage them to bring in examples and analyze the types of symmetry. Can they analyze the examples in this chapter? Look for the smallest region that might be a motif, a region that has no horizontal or vertical symmetry. Then compare the pattern with the seven types on page 155.

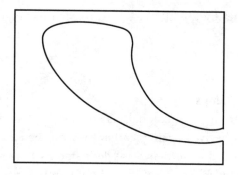

Code: H: flip about a horizontal axis
V: flip about a vertical axis

Type   Motion of stencil from one frame to the next

	1 to 2	2 to 3	3 to 4	4 to 5
1	slide	repeat	repeat	repeat
2	half-turn	repeat	repeat	repeat
3	H-flip and slide	repeat	repeat	repeat
4	V-flip	half-turn	V-flip	half-turn
5	V-flip	repeat	repeat	repeat
6	H-flip	V-flip	H-flip	V-flip
7	H-flip	slide	H-flip	slide

REPEATING PATTERNS IN THE PLANE

Block Prints—*Adinkra*

Young children will enjoy making block prints in a free style before they do more formal work. *Adinkra* cloth is worn by the Asante (also spelled Ashanti) people of Ghana. The cloth consists of a number of rectangles sewed together, with colorful borders separating the pieces. Each rectangle is stamped with rows of a different motif, each with its own symbolism. A motif is cut into a piece of a calabash attached to a handle, which is then dipped into ink or paint.

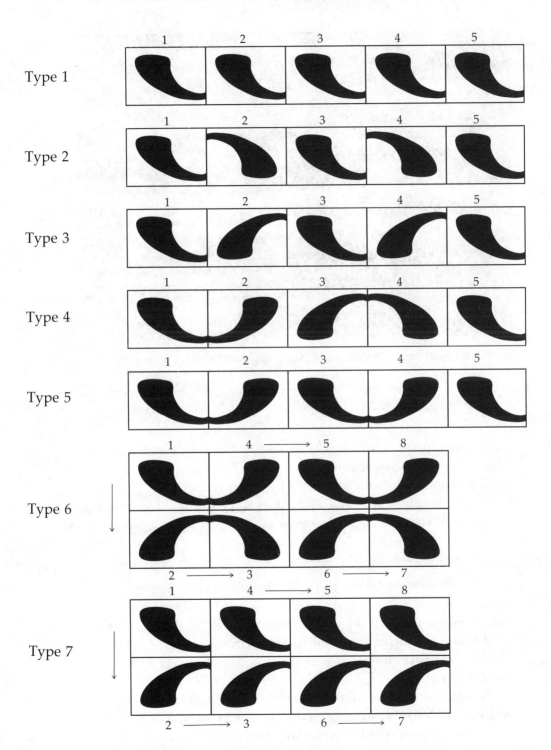

∎ **FIGURE 9–5 Repeated patterns in Hungarian embroidery. Photograph by Sam Zaslavsky**

Activities

Suggest that students or groups of students design their own motifs and print *adinkra*-like rectangles on paper or cloth. Paste or sew colored strips to connect the rectangles. Students should research the significance of *adinkra* and write about their art production from both the mathematical and cultural point of view.

Tessellations

A brick wall, a checkerboard, and a tiled bathroom floor are two examples of *tessellations*, repeated patterns that completely fill a space with no overlapping. The basic design element may be a triangle, a four-sided figure, a hexagon, or a combination of several shapes. The artist Maurits Escher used irregular figures in an amazingly clever way to tessellate a surface.

Perhaps the most celebrated example of tessellations is the art associated with the Islamic religion. Originating in the Middle East early in the seventh century, Islam spread rapidly through Turkey, North

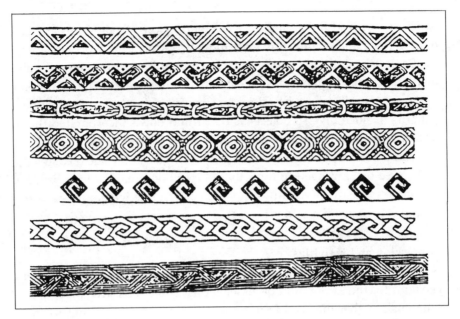

■ FIGURE 9–6 Seven border patterns, Kuba (Zaire)

■ FIGURE 9–7 Adinkra cloth, Asante (Ghana). Photograph by Sam Zaslavsky

Africa, Spain, and India, and later to other regions. Beautiful examples of Islamic art and architecture exist in many parts of the world.

Some Islamic sects forbade the depiction of human or animal forms in art. The most frequent design elements were geometric figures, floral designs, and calligraphy based on maxims from the Koran. Decorative patterns on such diverse objects as books and bowls incorporated these design elements. The inner and outer walls of mosques, palaces, and other important buildings were covered with glazed mosaic tiles in brilliant colors, arranged to form these typical designs. Patterns based entirely on construction with compass and straightedge emphasized the central role of geometry in art.

Discussion and activities

Shapes that tessellate. Pattern blocks and similar materials are an excellent medium for the exploration of tessellations. After some free play, ask students whether they can form tessellations using only triangles, only squares, only diamonds (rhombus), and so on, for each of the available shapes.

Have they found any shapes that do not tessellate? [All pattern blocks tessellate.]

Can they form tessellations with a combination of two shapes, such as the equilateral triangle and the regular hexagon?

Students can make tracings of their tessellations with single shapes and with combinations, so that they can analyze them later. They should keep a record of their conclusions and discuss them with the class.

Angle measurement. Ask students to make a tessellation with each of the following shapes, in turn: equilateral triangles, squares, and regular hexagons. They may use pattern blocks and trace them or draw on grid paper. Use square grid paper for squares and triangular grids (isometric paper) for triangles and hexagons.

Examine one point at which all the polygons meet. What is the sum of the angles at that point? [360°.]

How many polygons meet at that point? What is the measure of each angle in the polygon? Why do these shapes tessellate? [Triangle: 6, 60°; square: 4, 90°; hexagon: 3, 120°; 60, 90, and 120 are divisors of 360.]

■ **FIGURE 9–8 Islamic tessellations**

Why is it not possible to tessellate with regular pentagons (five-sided polygons)? [Each angle measures 108°, which is not a divisor of 360°.]

Make a tessellation using both equilateral triangles and regular hexagons. Find the sum of the angles around any point at which several polygons meet. Is it 360°?

Create tessellations. Children can draw their original designs on identical squares or rectangles. Mount them on a large sheet of posterboard to form a tessellation (this is similar to making a patchwork quilt). On another occasion use identical parallelograms or triangles as the basic design elements.

Polygons that tessellate. Students can investigate in a systematic way the types of polygons that tessellate. For example, do all triangles tessellate, regardless of the length of their sides or the size of their angles? [Yes; the sum of their angles is 180°, and 180 is a divisor of 360.] What types of quadrilaterals tessellate? [All; the sum of their angles is 360°.]

Students should record their conclusions and be prepared to defend them by drawing illustrations or by offering a counterexample—that is, demonstrate with a shape that does not tessellate, no matter how it is rotated. This is a good project for group work. Often a student who is not considered "good in math" can offer insights based on a feeling for geometry and art.

Create tessellations. As always, students can create their own tessellations, drawing inspiration from photographs of Islamic art, from the work of Maurits Escher, or other sources. The computer can be used as a tool. See *The Mathematics of Islamic Art* (Metropolitan Museum of Art) in "Other Resources." Students should experiment with designs that can be created with only a compass and straightedge, the tools used by Islamic artists. Coloring the pattern brings out the design elements.

Chapter 10

Data Analysis & the Culture of the Community

Mathematical Topics
Computation, measurement, large numbers, fractions, percentages, averages, estimation and approximation, graphing, pattern analysis, graph theory (trees).

Cultural Connections
Students' communities.

Linked Subjects
Genealogy, environment, smoking and health, quality of life, demographics.

People are most interested in the issues that are closest to them. What better way to demonstrate the power of mathematics than to show how it helps make sense of the world and points to ways to resolve their problems?

Some issues are common to most people, while others are specific to certain communities. Often communities disagree and actually clash over the means of resolving these issues. A good example, one that involves not only school children and parents, but all branches of government— legislatures, governors, and the courts—is the question of school finances. Some schools have beautiful facilities, hundreds of computers, and well-equipped laboratories, while others are housed in decrepit buildings and have few resources. As a consequence, many low-income students are deprived of an adequate education. Equalizing the funding for all schools in this era of tight budgets generally means the Robin

161

Hood approach—taking from the rich to give to the poor. Conflict is the inevitable result. Students might analyze the issue of school finance on a local level and plan appropriate actions to obtain their fair share or to share their largesse with needier schools.

Another issue that affects all of us is the preservation of the environment, saving our planet Earth and its resources. But even on this vital problem considerable disagreement arises. Citizens of some low-income and predominantly "minority" communities claim that toxic waste dumps and similar dangerous facilities are located disproportionately in their areas, a practice known as "environmental racism."

Gloria Ladson-Billings (1995) describes the plan of action and the mathematical involvement of a group of Puerto Rican students intent on removing a toxic waste dump from their low-income New York City neighborhood (129). I'll cite a specific example of environmental racism in my community. Several years ago a sewage-treatment plant was constructed along the Hudson River bordering Harlem, a center of African American life in New York City, in spite of vigorous protests on the part of the community. The plant had originally been planned for a different site, but the residents, predominantly white, were successful in warding it off. Since the construction, residents of the neighborhood have suffered from the unbearable odors given off by the plant. I live about three miles from the site, and when I drive past I must hold my nose, even with the car windows closed. Currently the community is waging a campaign to modify the plant procedures, an expensive proposition at this point. If the original plans had been carried out, odors might not be a problem. But, penny wise and pound foolish, the plans were modified to save a relatively small sum of money, resulting in a problem that is costly to correct.

Another hot issue is smoking. When the New York City Council Health Committee conducted hearings on a bill to ban smoking in most public places, lobbying both for and against the bill was intense. Philip Morris Companies, the world's largest cigarette maker, even threatened to move its headquarters out of New York City if the legislation passed. How does smoking affect our health, both directly and through breathing the secondhand smoke created by smokers in the immediate environment? How do tobacco companies like Philip Morris influence children to smoke?

Other issues are less controversial on a broad scale, although they may arouse strong feelings in individuals. How much television should children watch? Should school cafeterias serve the junk foods that so many children seem to prefer? (A good source of information on junk foods is KAJF [Kids Against Junk Food], c/o CSPI [Center for Science in the Public Interest], 1875 Connecticut Avenue, Washington, DC 20009, (202) 332-9110.)

Such issues are vital to the health and well-being of the students and the community. By discussing them, by collecting and analyzing relevant data, children become involved in problems that are important to them. They see that there can be more than one point of view. Such discussions encourage divergent thinking, the ability to see issues through the eyes of others. Students may or may not agree on a course of action. Whatever they do, they are learning the power of mathematics to help people understand the world, and they are learning to take responsibility for their lives.

Data analysis involves many aspects of math. Students must focus on and sort out the relevant data. They may have to do research to dig out more information. They develop a number sense, a feel for numbers, as they compare sets of data. Estimation and approximation skills improve as they perform necessary measurements and compute with the resulting numbers. They learn various ways to represent data in comprehensible and attractive forms. Most of all, they learn to solve real problems.

Another plus for bringing such issues into the curriculum is the wonderful opportunity it affords to work with parents and with the community. The benefits work both ways—parents become active partners in their children's mathematical education, while students learn how they can use math to change their lives and improve the larger society.

HERITAGE AND GENEALOGY

On a personal level, students might investigate their own heritage. Third and fourth graders at the Luis Muñoz Marin School in Brooklyn use technology for this purpose. According to the New York State *Technology Applications Quarterly* (1994), these students "demonstrated a multicultural, multimedia data base which [they] designed as a research and reference resource on family heritage. Each of the students showed how the data base can be accessed to provide a variety of information—text, graphics, video, and sound—on family histories, countries of origin, cultural traditions, ethnic food recipes, and national anthems, songs, and dances" (23).

Students can research their family connections and draw tree diagrams to illustrate their ancestry and relationships, a branch of mathematics called graph theory. They can compile tables and draw graphs to illustrate the states and countries from which their ancestors came. They might enjoy reading Lila Perl's *The Great Ancestor Hunt* (1994).

Students can compute how many ancestors they have going back three generations, then four and five generations, and so on. They can list these numbers in a table to show the number of ancestors for each generation and the total number of ancestors. What patterns do they see? Can they write a general expression for the total number of ancestors going back n generations, or an approximate number going back to year one? Genealogy is a wonderful activity to engage students and their families while they learn useful and interesting math.

A few words of caution, though: Students may not be living with both, or even one parent. Some children are adopted and may not know much about their biological parents. The project should be phrased in such a way as to allow all students to be comfortable with it.

SAVE THE ENVIRONMENT

Trash and Garbage

"Talking Trash with the Environmental Rebuilders" is the title of a pamphlet I picked up at the street fair celebrating the conclusion of a summer program at a local middle school, Salomé Ureña Middle Academies (IS 218M), a New York City public school. Here are excerpts from the introduction by eighth-grader Jaydean Testa:

> The program that I go to is called Summer of Service. Summer of Service is a national program where kids learn and try to help themselves and their community. . . . The New York City

program is helping to make the environment a better place for
people to live in. The program is really interesting. The
program is also fun and exciting. . . .

There are five houses which help organize the program.
There are five teams in each house. A team is made up of eight
kids and two co-mentors. Let me give you some examples of
team names: Junk Busters, and the Environmental Rebuilders.

Each team has its own project. For example, my team is
doing a project about recycling. Recycling is a good way to
reduce pollution and a good way to help keep the environment
clean. We are creating a pamphlet for people to read at the
street fair. During the summer, team 1A and other teams
cleaned a lot behind P.S. 5 [a new elementary school].

The members of the team wrote short articles about recyclable
materials: paper, metal, plastic, and glass. Then followed tips on
recycling and the recycling days in Manhattan (with a map), a poem, a
"Recycling Word Search," a concluding story ("What Would Happen If
We Didn't Recycle?"), and brief biographies of the team members and
co-mentors. Although applications to mathematics did not appear in the
pamphlet, I know that the children, aged ten to fourteen, did use math
in the course of their activities.

In their book *Read Any Good Math Lately?* (1992), Whitin and Wilde
describe several classroom experiences based on the book *50 Simple
Things Kids Can Do to Save the Earth* (EarthWorks Group 1990). Using the
statistics on pollution contained in this book, students were motivated to
initiate their own investigations into conserving water, recycling cans,
using plastic packaging materials, and disposing of organic garbage.
These are issues that involve every family, as well as the school, and
enable children to apply global data to their own problems.

The following activity contributed to the title of Susan Ohanian's
Garbage Pizza, Patchwork Quilts, and Math Magic (1992). On page 59 she
describes how Patricia Hale has her students examine their garbage at
home. "Then they make cardboard pizzas, depicting percentages of
waste in a pie graph: paper gets the largest slice, followed by yard
waste, food, metals, glass, and plastics. Students decorate their pizzas
with samples of the appropriate trash, so that instead of pepperoni, they
have pieces of old newspaper, weeds, M & M's, and so on. These pizzas

make a graphic display in the hallway, testimony to students as researchers and problem solvers."

If your students have not yet learned to make the circle graphs called for in the Garbage Pizza activity, here is a method that does not require a knowledge of central angles. Give each student a strip of paper one meter in length. He or she colors the sections of the strip to represent the percentages (or fractions) for each type of waste. All the students can then join the ends of their strips to form a circle for the graph from which they can learn about the measurement of central angles.

Water Conservation

Whitin and Wilde (1992, 4–5) describe a second-grade classroom's project to estimate how much water they could conserve by turning off the tap while brushing their teeth. First they had to gather data: How many minutes do people spend brushing their teeth? Two, on the average. How often do they brush? Twice a day. How much water pours out of the tap in two minutes? The students measured, and found that the answer was three gallons of water for each brushing, or six gallons a day for each person. Then they found that they needed only one cup of water for a brushing; all the rest of the three gallons was wasted, right down the drain.

In the course of this experiment, children collected information, they gained some understanding of the word *average*, they learned about units of measurement and how to use them, they performed arithmetic operations with real data, and they used calculators to arrive at solutions. Most important, they used mathematics as a tool to solve real problems.

This experiment can be extended in many ways. Before they begin to collect data, students might "guesstimate" the answers—come up with an educated guess based on their experience. Suppose the water runs at a faster or a slower rate? They might compute the savings over a period of a week or a year, for the class and for the school, and learn about rounding off large numbers; after all, the figures they are using are only approximations. They should understand that no measurement is exact, no matter how precise the tools used to measure. Graphs of their results provide an instant picture of the data, and they can present their findings in poster form.

Students might compile their individual "Water Diaries." How much water does each family use every day or every week for baths and showers, to flush the toilet, to wash dishes? How can such quantities be measured? Can these quantities be reduced? See *50 Simple Things Kids Can Do to Save the Earth* (EarthWorks Group 1990) for good ideas on how to carry out such a project.

On a broader scale, students might investigate the source of their local water supply. Is the supply adequate all year round? How does the amount of rainfall affect the supply? Some newspapers carry daily information about the status of the local water supply. The *New York Times*, for example, gives daily figures as follows: water level in local reservoirs on the preceding day as a percentage of maximum, the estimated normal level (average for that date computed over a number of years), and the consumption in billions of gallons on the preceding day.

Once they are aware of some of the issues, students might discuss the kind of action they can undertake to solve the problems: design posters for the school and the community, write letters to government officials and the local newspaper, interview people involved with this issue. Some communities are challenging the authorities on the grounds that their sources of water have been diverted to other uses. Native American groups, in particular, have been deprived of both their water supply and the fish that furnish their sustenance.

Recycling Cans and Bottles

Whitin and Wilde (1992, 61–62) tell how Rick DuVall's fifth-grade class used the information in *50 Simple Things Kids Can Do to Save the Earth* as a starting point for a project on recycling cans. Knowing that recycling one aluminum can instead of manufacturing a new one saves enough electricity to run a television set for three hours, the children kept diaries on the time they spent watching TV. Further research led them to the conclusion that the families of the children in the class used about 185,000 cans a year. If all these cans were recycled, how many hours could a television set run on the electricity saved? Further, are the data in *50 Simple Things* reasonable? Whitin and Wilde point out the discrepancy between a total of 65 billion cans used annually in the United States and the figure of 1,500 cans per person, a number that is too high by a factor of six. Students can be challenged to determine which number is more accurate.

In *The Black Snowman* (Mendez 1989), discussed in Chapter 3, the little boy tries to earn money by collecting cans and bottles. Now we know that we can also save electricity by recycling cans. Your students will probably think of other ways to apply math to this topic. Books like *50 Simple Things Kids Can Do to Save the Earth* are full of ideas.

Data Analysis Methodology

"Paper Profits" is the title of an op-ed piece in the *New York Times* (12 February 1994) by Iowa teacher Joan Braunagel McShane. I will use her description to present a methodology for the analysis of data.

1. Students raise a question. The project started when a sixth grader described the chaos in his home the previous night: clogged toilet, flowing sewage, call for a plumber. The cause was huge amounts of tissue.
2. Students develop conjectures. Why would tissue cause such a problem? What factors determine the type of tissue people buy?
3. The class designs an investigation. A real toilet was brought into the classroom, along with a 56-liter waste basket full of water and a sump pump. Students collected 43 brands of tissue.
4. Students collect data. They designed data sheets and set up testing stations. They noted such features as weight, strength, odor, etc., and recorded their data. They invited community experts to assist them.
5. Students present their results.
6. Students interpret their findings. They determined that one brand was superior: it broke up best and retained the least water.

McShane concludes: "The students—58 percent of them nonwhite, 85 percent from low-income families—have learned that they can be contributing members of the community, and learned that science can help them solve problems every day and everywhere. My students are continuously involved in other projects that concern issues in their community. . . . After 30 years of teaching, my claim to fame is 'Toilet Queen of Davenport, Iowa.' It's a title I accept with pride."

SMOKING[1]

Background

As a nonsmoker and an asthmatic whose father was also asthmatic, I am delighted by the campaigns to restrict smoking. So it was with pleasure that I saw in the local press a photograph of a parade of elementary and middle school children carrying "No Smoking" signs and a coffin in which to bury a model of Joe Camel. Studies show that half of all smokers start their habit before the age of thirteen, and that even six-year-olds are as familiar with Joe Camel as with Mickey Mouse. From 1988 to 1992, profits from the sale of Camels soared from $6 million to $476 million ("Tobacco Industry Seeks New Recruits" 1993).

Tobacco is a slow killer. Although the percentage of adults who smoke has declined considerably during the past few decades (see graph), deaths from smoking-related causes have risen sharply. In a 1991 report by the National Centers for Disease Control, Dr. William L. Roper, director of the Centers, stated: "The problem is, we are now paying for what happened twenty or thirty years ago, when large numbers of people smoked in large amounts ("Death Toll from Smoking Is Worsening"). Lung cancer now kills more women than breast cancer. Tobacco use is responsible for one fifth of all deaths in America. Here are some figures for deaths from smoking:

---

[1] *Statistics on smoking are from the following sources:*

Action on Smoking and Health. 1991. ASH Smoking and Health Review. (March–April): 6.

"Death Toll from Smoking Is Worsening." 1991. New York Times (February 1): A14.

Leary, W. E. "Surgeon General Urges Banning Cigarette Ads Aimed at the Young." 1994. New York Times (February 25): A12.

"Secondhand Smoke Assailed in Report." 1991. New York Times (May 30): A22.

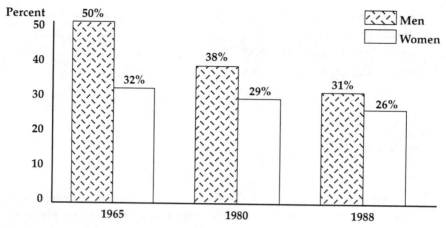

■ FIGURE 10–1 Percent of population who smoked cigarettes

1965: 30,000 women; 158,000 men; 188,000 total.
1988: 147,000 women; 287,000 men; 434,000 total.

Recent reports show that people may also suffer from other people's smoking, called "secondhand smoke." The U.S. Surgeon General's office estimates that 53,000 people die every year from exposure to tobacco smoke of others. Young children are particularly vulnerable to smoke in the environment.

In 1992 the tobacco companies spent almost $4 billion on advertising. Much of this advertising is directed to low-income communities, young people, people of color, and women. In 1992 and 1993 smoking rose among people under the age of eighteen, after a decline.

Here is how a group of sixth graders responded to the tobacco ads that appear on billboards in sports stadiums. Awarded free tickets to the New York Mets game for winning the club's Team Up for the Environment contest, they were so shocked by what they saw that they wrote letters to the Mets to protest. Danielle Scheafer wrote: "When we arrived at our seats we noticed a big sign for Marlboro cigarettes. This sign shows up all the time as it is near the scoreboard." Although ads for cigarettes are banned from television, these stadium ads appear on the screen.

Discussion and Activities

1. Contact the U.S. Department of Health & Human Services, Centers for Disease Control and Prevention, Office of Smoking and Health (telephone 1-800-CDC-1311). The following materials are available free of charge:

• "SGR 4 KIDS: The Surgeon General's Report for Kids About Smoking" (1994). Facts about smoking, interviews with children and with the Surgeon General, actions that students have taken in all parts of the United States, ten ways you can help to make your world smoke free.

• "It's Time to Stop Being a Passive Victim" (1993). Facts about secondhand smoke, statistics on cigarette use and advertising.

2. Contact SmokeFree Educational Services, Inc., 375 South End Avenue, Suite 32F, New York, NY 10280-1085; telephone (212) 912-0960; Fax (212) 488-8911. This organization publishes information on health statistics and actions taken and sponsors campaigns such as poster contests. To join and receive the quarterly newsletter *SmokeFree Air* and other materials, send $25 or a copy of a letter to a person targeted in the newsletter. You can probably receive one issue free of charge. (The story and letter about the New York Mets are from the Fall 1993 issue.)

3. Discuss with children the kind of life they expect to be leading thirty years hence. Will that life include smoking? Then bring in some facts about tobacco for students. Encourage them to collect data on smoking in their homes and community.

4. Have students discuss and analyze some of the figures about smoking. Do men or women do better in cutting down on smoking? Help them see the numbers in terms of their own lives.

See Davidman and Davidman (1994, 108–20) for an interdisciplinary sequence of lessons on smoking prevention.

■ **FIGURES 10–2A & B Two posters from** *Kids Say Don't Smoke* **(Melissa Antonow, grade 5, and Caheim Drake, grade 4)**

QUALITY OF LIFE

Background

There are many ways to measure the quality of life of a society. Two of the most important are infant mortality and life expectancy. The *infant mortality rate* tells how many babies die before their first birthday, for every 1,000 live births. Another common method to measure the well-being of young children is to compute the number of deaths of children under age five, per 1,000 live births. *Life expectancy* tells the average age at which people in a certain population die. Poverty and racism affect both these indicators.

Infant mortality

In 1992 the rate for the United States was nine deaths per 1,000 live births. Twenty-one countries did better; Japan led with a rate of four. At the other end, with rates of almost 200 deaths for every 1,000 live births, were the African countries Niger, Mozambique, and Angola. When we compare the rates for blacks and whites in the United States, we find that black babies die at more than twice the rate of white babies. The black infant mortality rate was higher than the overall rates of forty-one other countries.

Life expectancy

In 1992 life expectancy in the United States was 76 years, about the same as Cuba, Israel, and Austria. Leading the list was Japan with a life expectancy of 79 years. To come back to the United States, the figure of 76 years conceals many discrepancies. Women live longer than men by about seven years. Whites live about six years longer than blacks. American Indians have the shortest life span of any ethnic/racial group.

These statistics come from two excellent sources of information on many aspects of the quality of life, both published annually: *The State of the World's Children* (United Nations Children's Fund [UNICEF]), and *The State of America's Children* (Children's Defense Fund [CDF]). The latter gives figures for every state and large city. The United States Bureau of the Census will send kits of materials designed for students in grades K–12. See "Other Resources" for addresses. An almanac also gives useful information.

In its June 1992 update of the pamphlet "Census Bureau Education Program," the Bureau lists ways in which its findings can help students in mathematics, science, social studies, and language arts. For mathematics, students will:

- Develop number sense and computational skills.
- Recognize the use of mathematics in everyday life and in other curriculum areas.
- Collect and organize data and apply descriptive statistics.
- Interpret displays of data with tables, maps, and graphs.
- Use models, facts, and relationships to explain their thinking and explore independent, dependent, and mutually exclusive phenomena/events.

Discussion and Activities

Students might survey the class on several aspects of the quality of life. How do they spend their own lives? One popular survey topic is the number of hours spent watching television. Bob Peterson, fifth-grade teacher at the Fratney School in Milwaukee, discusses such a project in his article, "Teaching for Social Justice: One Teacher's Journey" (Bigelow et al. 1994):

> In math we learn about percentages, fractions, graphing, and basic math through using numbers to examine their own lives. For example, my fifth-grade class keeps logs of the time that they spend watching television, graph it, and analyze it in terms of fractions and percentages. . . . I tried to take the activity a step further—not only to affirm what's going on in the children's lives, but to help them question if watching television is always in their best interests. As we looked at television viewing, for instance, we found that some of our students could save over 1,000 hours a year by moderating their TV watching.
>
> "I can't believe I waste so much time watching TV," one girl stated during a discussion.
>
> "You're not wasting it," replied one boy. "You're learning what they want you to buy!" he said sarcastically. (31–32)

Peterson encourages his students to analyze programs for violence and for bias against women and ethnic groups and to keep tallies. How often are certain people, viewpoints, or groups presented in the media?

Depending on the students' grade level and maturity, they can become involved in research dealing with quality of life and social justice issues. Here are some suggestions:

1. UNICEF's "Trick or Treat" program encourages young people to collect funds for needy children worldwide. Even young children can relate to the fact that a ten-cent-per-child treatment can save the lives every year of more than a million children suffering from diarrheal disease.

2. How might students account for the differences in infant mortality between blacks and whites, or the longer life span of women, compared with men? From the mathematical point of view, why aren't infant mortality rates given as percentages?

3. To introduce the topic of percentage, represent a total population as one hundred people. Children can visualize twenty children out of a hundred, or one out of five, living in poverty in the United States.

4. Besides population figures for states, cities, and smaller areas, the Census Bureau publishes statistics on such factors as educational level, type of housing, and income. See "Multicultural Mathematics: One Road to the Goal of Mathematics for All" (Zaslavsky 1993b) for a description of lessons based on such data.

The demographics of the United States are changing rapidly. The Census Bureau traces changes in the population by ethnic and racial categories and publishes reports on the characteristics of the different groups.

1. Included in the Census Bureau kit is a 1990 Census Profile, "Race and Hispanic Origin." It traces the changes in the population from 1960 to 1990. Students might investigate the connection between the rapid growth of the Hispanic population (a result, in part, of immigration) and the high rates of infant mortality and poverty in Latin American countries.

2. Another interesting issue is the size of the American Indian, Eskimo, and Aleut population, which has increased from a little over half a million in 1960 to nearly two million in 1990. What factors account for this surge? One possible reason is that Native American people are more willing than formerly to acknowledge their heritage.

3. An even more interesting question is the estimation that in the pre-European period as many as ten million Native Americans may have lived in the present United States and Canada. How do we account for these drastic changes? What role was played by conquest and by European-introduced diseases? Not only are students dealing with numbers as they research the answers to such questions, but they are also overcoming a stereotypical view about the history of the Native Peoples in the development of the United States.

 *Chapter 11*

Games of Many Cultures

■ **Mathematical Topics**
Critical thinking, number sense, computation, geometry, measurement, probability, combinatorics.

Cultural Connections
Many cultures.

Linked Subjects
Archaeology, anthropology, history, geography, art.

Background: Why Play Games?

This chapter discusses games, puzzles, and recreational activities from many cultures. I have chosen activities that are common to more than one society and that go back centuries, even millennia. Among them are river-crossing puzzles, three-in-a-row and other games of position, *mankala* (or *mancala*), games of chance, and networks.

Why play games in the mathematics class? First of all, because they are fun. Games engage students' interest by challenging them, either to win against an opponent or to complete an interesting task. In connection with the outcomes when throwing dice, Bell and Cornelius (1988) comment, "It was interesting to observe that pupils would carry out some quite complex analyses when given tasks which were based on a game but that they would be less willing and less interested to carry out the same tasks in isolation" (96). An editor from the Philippines told me that she had learned more mathematics from playing the game *sungka*, a version of mankala, than she had learned in her school math classes.

Some of these activities—networks, for example—may be considered games in our culture but have deeper significance in other societies. The Chokwe people of Angola have a tradition of drawing network diagrams in the sand to illustrate proverbs, fables, games, riddles, and history, an integral part of the education of the community. I presented some of these activities to a ninth-grade social studies class and asked for their evaluations. One boy, an outstanding math student (he was in an eleventh-grade math class), wrote that the network activity was pleasant recreation but could hardly be considered "real math." His stereotypical view of "real math" was shaped by the school curriculum—standard algebra and geometry proofs. Yet the mathematical principles involved in drawing these networks are closely related to significant problems in our society, such as devising the most efficient routes for collecting garbage in cities.

I often come across these games in Americanized versions. A game called Wild Goose Chase, published in Scholastic's *Math Power* magazine (September 1, 1991), is actually the traditional Maori game *mu torere*. Mankala games have appeared under such names as Pitfall and Kalah.

Most of the activities develop skill in problem solving by requiring students to work out strategies, to think ahead, and to evaluate various moves. Children exercise their skills in geometry and measurement as they draw "boards" for the games of position. Mankala games help students develop their number sense and offer practice in computation. Games of chance introduce concepts of probability and combinatorial mathematics as students try to predict outcomes when tossing coins or spinning tops.

Activities

Certain types of activities are appropriate for most of the games and puzzles presented here. Here are some examples. Students might:

1. Teach the game, perhaps in a simplified version, to younger children. They can prepare an illustrated manual to help children learn the game.
2. Research the customs associated with a game. Is it played by children or adults, by men or women, on special occasions or on ordinary days?

3. Analyze the game and work out strategies for winning.
4. Change the rules of the game, the type of board, the number of players, the number of counters, or any other features. How do these changes affect the strategies?

RIVER-CROSSING PUZZLES

Background

River-crossing puzzles have been traced back to an eighth-century letter to the Emperor Charlemagne from his teacher, Alcuin of York. No doubt they were based on real transportation problems and formed part of the oral traditions of many societies.

In one version, from the Sea Islands off the coast of South Carolina, a man has to carry a fox, a duck, and a sack of corn across a river. His boat can hold only two objects besides the man himself. The man cannot leave the fox with the duck because the fox loves duck meat. And if he leaves the corn with the duck, the duck will devour the whole sack. How did the man get the fox, the duck, and the corn to the other side of the river? What is the minimum number of round trips?

In another version with a similar cast of characters, the boat can carry only one object besides the man. How can the man get his cargo across with the fewest number of trips? Does he make more or fewer trips than in the previous version?

These are the simplest versions of this age-old puzzle, told in many parts of the world. In Liberia the puzzle involves a man, a leopard, a goat, and a bundle of cassava leaves. Other versions involve three jealous husbands and their wives, masters and servants, and merchants and robbers. Common to all is the prohibition on leaving certain characters with certain other characters.

Discussion and Activities

Role play
Crossing-the-river puzzles offer a wonderful opportunity for children to solve a problem by acting out the situation. After a discussion of the puzzle and possible solutions, divide the class into groups of four. Each child plays a different character, identified by signs or whatever devices the students choose. By trial and error they will arrive at a solution,

perhaps with a bit of help. They should make notes on their plan of action so that they will know what works and what doesn't. Is there more than one solution?

Research
Adapt the puzzles to other geographic regions or periods in history, based on research on animals and their eating habits.

Writing
Write about and illustrate solutions to the puzzles.

Complexity
Make the puzzles more complex by adding one or two characters to the cast. Students should record and analyze the solutions that work and those that don't work, a good exercise in logic and in communication.

THREE-IN-A-ROW GAMES

All the games described here require fairly simple boards that the students can construct themselves, using their skills in geometry and measurement.

Background and Rules of Play

Children in the United States play *tic-tac-toe*. In England the game is called *naughts and crosses*. It is one of the simplest and most recent forms of the three-in-a-row games that are popular from Iceland to the southern tip of Africa. Over a hundred years ago, scientists examining the 3,300-year-old temple to the Egyptian Pharaoh Sethos I found strange diagrams carved into the rooftop slabs. These diagrams are similar to the game boards used today for some three-in-a-row games. It seems that they were carved by the workmen who put up the building, perhaps to squeeze in a fast game during their lunch break.

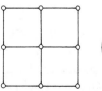 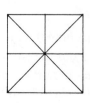 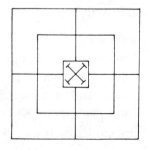

How did these games reach so many parts of the world? Ancient Greek scholars spent years in Egypt, a center of culture and learning. Perhaps the Romans learned these games from the Greeks and spread them when they conquered Europe, the Middle East, and North Africa. By that time the Chinese and other Asian peoples had been playing these games for centuries. Game diagrams were often carved on the tops of stone walls and the steps of buildings, and are still visible in many parts of the world. In 1989 an inspector noticed a one-foot-square game board for *nine men's morris* that had been carved under the staircase to the cellar in the eighteenth-century farmhouse known as Dyckman House, in northern New York City, now a historic monument. Other people had noticed it but, unfamiliar with the game, had paid no attention.

All three-in-a-row games are for two players (or two teams) playing against each other. Each player has a specified number of counters—checkers or beans or plastic disks. One player has one color, and the other player has a different color. (I use white and black here, although the counters may be of any color or type, as long as they are distinguishable.) As the name implies, the object is to place three counters in a straight line, with no empty points between them, before the opponent can do so. I will describe four versions of the game: *shisima* from western Kenya, *tapatan* from the Philippines, *nine men's morris* from England, and *nerenchi* from Sri Lanka. Every book of board games includes at least one version of the game. It is often called *three* (*five, six, nine, or twelve*) *men's morris,* the number indicating the number of counters for each player.

The most complex version that I have encountered is *murabaraba,* played with twenty-four counters in Lesotho (southern Africa). An instructor in Lesotho conducted a controlled experiment with seventh-grade students and found that those who knew the game tested significantly better on certain standardized geometry questions.

Shisima

A colleague from western Kenya told me that he had played the game as a small child. He and his friends drew the game board in the sand on the bank of a stream and used pebbles as playing pieces. When I informed him that the game was available commercially in the United States, he was surprised and thrilled to know that his culture was recognized.

Shisima means "body of water," and the counters are called *imbalivali*, or water bugs, because they move so rapidly around the game board. Each player has three counters. The game board is in the shape of an octagon with the shisima in the center.

How to play. The game is played on the eight points where lines intersect, plus the shisima. The game opens with each player's counters placed as in the diagram. Player One moves a white counter along a line to the next empty point. Then Player Two moves a black counter one space along a line to an empty point. A player may move into the center, or shisima, at any time. Jumping over a counter is not allowed.

Finish. The first player to place all three imbalavali in a straight line is the winner. There are four ways to get three-in-a-row; they all go through the shisima. The game ends in a draw when the same set of moves has been repeated three times.

Tapatan

Some Philippine families kept beautiful wooden game boards for *tapatan*, while others had the diagrams marked on the floors or doorsteps of their homes. They used special round counters, three of light wood for one player and three of dark wood for the other player. The game board is a square with interior lines, as in the diagram. The game is played on the nine points where lines intersect.

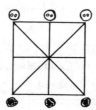

How to play. Players take turns going first. Player One places a white counter on any point. Then Player Two places a black counter on any empty point. They take turns until all the counters are on the board. Player One moves one of his or her counters along a line to the next empty point. Jumping over a counter is not allowed. Then Player Two moves one of his or her counters along a line to the next vacant point. They continue to take turns.

Finish. The winner is the first person to make a row of three in a straight line. There are eight different ways to make a row: three across, three down, and two along the diagonal. If neither player can make a row of three, the game is called a draw. The game ends in a draw when the same set of moves has been repeated three times and it is obvious that neither player can win.

Other games played according to the rules for tapatan, and the countries in which they are played, are listed below. Some versions omit the diagonal lines on the board, but still allow three-in-a-row along the diagonals.

El-Qirqat	Arabic-speaking countries
Three Men's Morris	English-speaking countries
Marelle Assise	France
Achi	Ghana and Nigeria (players may use four counters)
Hujura	Iran
Cashlan Gherra	Ireland
Filo; Mulino	Italy
Tres en Raya	Spain

Nine men's morris

This game, along with *three men's morris* and chess, was introduced into Spain from North Africa by Arabic-speaking Moors in the eighth century. Five hundred years later King Alfonso X included them in the Spanish *Book of Games*, the first European game book. The king wrote: "God has intended men to enjoy themselves with many games." No wonder he was called Alfonso the Wise! The name of the game, *alquerque de nueve* ("mill with nine"), is from the Arabic. *Alquerque* is also the name of part of the mill used to press oil from olives. The game spread to many European countries, where it is often called "mill." In his play *A Midsummer Night's Dream*, Shakespeare wrote: "The Nine Men's Morris is filled up with mud."

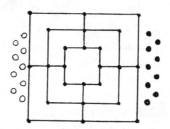

How to play. Each player has nine counters. The game board has twenty-four points of intersection. The directions correspond to those for tapatan. A row of three is called a mill. A player who makes a mill is allowed to remove one of the other player's counters from the board, and the captured counters are no longer in the game. However, a counter may not be removed from the opponent's mill, unless no other counter is on the board.

Finish. A player who has only two counters on the board or is unable to move has lost the game.

Below is a list of three-in-a-row games in which each player has nine counters, and the countries in which they are played.

Dris	Arabic-speaking countries
Trique	Colombia
Merelles	France
Muhle	Germany
Triodi	Greece
Malom	Hungary
Nao-guti	India
Yakamaido	Indians of California
Pitarilla; Picaría	Indians of Southwest United States
Mulinello	Italy
Akidada	Nigeria
Melnitsa	Russia
Qvarn	Sweden

Nerenchi

This game has long been a favorite of women and girls in Sri Lanka. Diagrams for three-in-a-row games were carved in temple steps two thousand years ago.

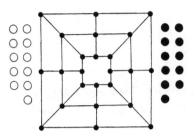

How to play. Each player has eleven counters. The game is played on the twenty-four intersection points, as in nine men's morris. The two players (or teams) take turns placing one counter at a time on an empty point on the board. A player who makes a row of three, called a *nerenchi,* during the "placing" stage gets an extra turn. A nerenchi is made along any of the lines marked on the board, including the diagonals.

The last player to place a counter on the board makes the first move. The players take turns moving one counter at a time along a line to the next empty point. Counters may *not* move along the diagonal lines. The object is to get as many nerenchi as possible. There are twenty possible ways to do this. A player who makes a nerenchi during the "moving" stage may remove any one of the opponent's counters.

Finish. The loser is the player or team that has lost all but two counters or is blocked from moving.

Below is a list of three-in-a-row games in which each player (or team) has twelve counters. The rules and the board may differ somewhat from those for nerenchi.

Thon-htap Kya	Myanmar (Burma)
Sam K'i	China
Kon-tjil	Korea
Dig Dig	Malaysia

Shah	Somalia
Murabaraba	Southern Africa
Twelve Men's Morris	United States, New England Colonies

Discussion and Activities

Tic-tac-toe

Ask students whether they know how to play *tic-tac-toe*. Children who know can teach those who don't. Depending on their maturity, encourage them to discuss strategies for winning. In every class there are some who want to show how smart they are. Try to control the situation so that no student is inhibited or made to feel "dumb."

Comparison

How are the games described above similar to tic-tac-toe? How are they different?

Geometry

Discuss the geometry of the game boards. Encourage students to design, make, and decorate boards for the games.

Analysis

For each game, how many ways are there to make three-in-a-row? Work out strategies for the game. Is the person who goes first more likely to win? Where should Player One place the first counter? Player Two?

Innovation

Encourage students to change the games by introducing variations in the number of counters, in the diagram for the board, or in the rules, and to write about the revised versions. That's how new games are invented.

Computer games

Computer-wise students may be able to program the computer to play some of the games. It's worth a try.

BLOCKING GAMES

Pong hau k'i

This is a simple game from China; in Korea it is called *ou-moul-ko-no*.

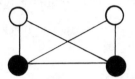

How to play. Each of the two players has two counters, one color for Player One and a different color for Player Two. The counters are placed on the board as in the diagram. Play is on the five intersecting points. Player One moves one counter into the center. Player Two moves a counter along a line to the empty point. They continue to take turns.

Finish. The game ends when one player is blocked from moving.

Mu torere

According to their traditions, the Maori people came to New Zealand in seven canoes. In the Maori language, which is related to those of Tahiti and Hawaii, this land is called Aotearoa. They play *mu torere* on a board that looks like an eight-pointed star, with a small circle in the center called the *putahi*. The points are called *kawai*. Drawing the board is a good exercise in geometry. The octagonal board for shisima will do just as well, perhaps even better, because the lines along which the counters move are clearly marked. The moves in both games are similar, but the object of each game is different.

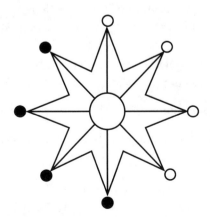

How to play. Each of the two players has four counters; one set is "white" and the other "black." To start, they are arranged as in the diagram. Black goes first. The players take turns moving their counters one at a time to an empty point or empty putahi. A counter may move into the putahi only if it is next to at least one of the opponent's counters. [Why?] Jumping over a counter is not allowed.

Finish. The winner is the player who can block the opponent from making any moves.

I call mu torere a three-in-a-corner game, because the winning formation is a right angle with an empty point between the two counters on the points of the star. This is the reason for the restriction on moving into the putahi. [Students should discover this formation for themselves.]

Discussion and Activities

Dr. Beverly Ferrucci introduces games and other cultural activities to the current and future teachers taking her courses at Keene State College, New Hampshire, and shared these two blocking games with me. She has developed sets of questions for her students to ponder as they play the games, as well as suggestions for further explorations. She challenged a group of middle school students to think about strategies in this way, and sent me their conclusions, shown in brackets after the questions. Many of the same questions apply also to three-in-a-row games.

Here are her questions for the games pong hau k'i and mu torere.

Questions to explore during the activity:

1. Is it best to go first? Explain. [Generally not.]
2. Can you win if you go second? Explain. [They worked out several ways.]
3. How many winning positions are there?
4. Identify the situation when you realized you had won or lost the game.
5. In your journal discuss the strategies you used when you played the game.

Further explorations:

1. Can you enlarge the board and play the same game? [Various answers.]

2. Do you have to change the rules or can you keep them the same? Explain. [Various answers.]
3. Can you use the same strategies? Explain. [Various answers.]

Additional explorations for mu torere:

4. Can you make the board smaller and play the same game? [Yes.]
5. Do you have to change the rules? Explain. [No.]
6. Can you use the same strategies? Explain. [Yes.]

MANKALA GAMES

Background

Mankala games are popular in most of Africa and in parts of Asia—India, Sri Lanka, Malaysia, Indonesia, some Arabic-speaking countries, central Asia, and the Philippines. Many years ago captives from Africa brought the game to Brazil, Suriname, and the Caribbean islands. The earliest known board dates back over three millennia to ancient Egypt, where several diagrams for the games were cut into stone in temples at Qurna, Karnak, and Luxor.

Here I will describe a version that is becoming popular in schools in the United States—*oware* (or *wari*) as played in Ghana and in Nigeria on a two-row board. Asian versions of the game also use the two-row board. In eastern and southern Africa the four-row board is popular, under such names as *bao, nchuba, mweso,* and *mangola*. A three-row version is played in Ethiopia. The game has as many sets of rules as it has names. It is based entirely on mathematical principles, and some experts rate it among the ten best games in the world.

The terms used in the game reflect the culture and history of the people who play that particular version. Some call the playing pieces "cattle," others "take prisoners" or "buy houses" or "fill the treasuries."

Oware

Oware (oh-war-ee) is played by the Asante people of Ghana. The Yoruba people of southwest Nigeria play *ayo* with similar rules. This is a game for two people or two teams. They sit facing each other, with the board between them. One side of the board belongs to Player One and the other side to Player Two. Some teachers have children learn on a "board" drawn on a large sheet of paper, so that they can follow the moves easily. If an authentic game board is not available, an egg carton will do nicely. The game is played with forty-eight beans, and each player should have a cup into which to place captured beans. This "endcup" is usually placed to the player's right.

To start. Distribute four beans into each hole.

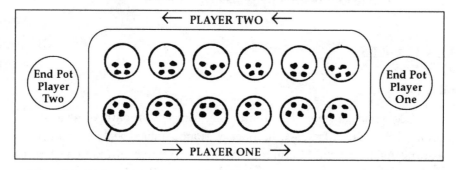

How to play. Player One picks up all the beans in any one of her six holes. She drops ("sows") one bean in each hole going around the board to her right (counterclockwise) until she has dropped all the beans. Player Two does the same, starting on his side of the board. They continue, taking turns. If a player picks up 12 or more beans from one cup, so that sowing the beans requires at least a complete cycle of the board, she skips the cup from which those beans were taken.

To capture. When the last bean dropped in a cup on the opponent's side of the board makes a group of two or three, those beans are captured. If the hole just before this last one also has two or three beans, they may be captured, and the same with the adjoining holes going backward (clockwise) on the opponent's side.

To finish. When one player has no beans left on his side, the other player must move so that she gives him some beans, if possible. If only one or two beans remain on the board, they go to the player whose side they are on. The player who has captured more beans is the winner.

Note that in *no* African version of the game are beans dropped into the endcups as they are sowed. However, in many Asian versions a player drops a bean into his or her endcup (but not in the opponent's) when sowing beans. See *Africa Counts* (Zaslavsky 1979, 116–36) for a discussion of the cultural aspects of this game.

Discussion and Activities

Simplify

To introduce young children to the game, use a smaller board and fewer beans—for example, a sheet of paper divided into two rows of four boxes, with two beans in each box. If the last bean in any move makes a group of two in a box on the opponent's side, these beans are placed in the player's endcup; the same with the box just before this one, continuing backward, capturing from the opponent's side of the board.

Bell and Cornelius (1988) suggest starting on a board with two rows of three holes, and two beans in each hole. Players sow from any cup. The winner is the first to get five beans in any hole.

Capture

Draw a game board on a transparency and set up a possible "capture" situation on the overhead projector. Students should discuss the best moves.

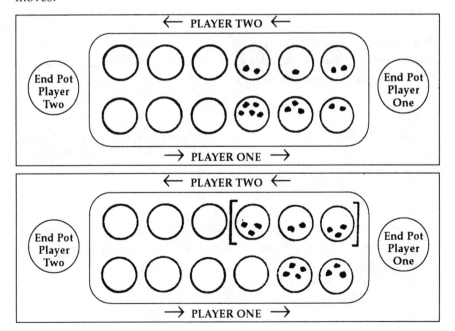

■ **FIGURE 11–1 Sixth graders Yadiris and Leo enjoy a game of oware.**
Photograph by Sam Zaslavsky

Innovation
Students might change the rules and try out the resulting game. An
alternative is to learn a new version.

Research
Encourage students to learn about the economy and history of the
people whose version they are playing. They should decorate their egg-
carton gameboards with symbols appropriate to the society.

Oware contest
Promote an oware contest in the class or school. Students might play in
teams, rather than as individuals. This competition can be part of a
cultural festival.

PROBABILITY GAMES

Background

The games that we have discussed are all based on the skill of the players, the ability to work out strategies. The outcomes in probability games rest on chance, on "the way the chips fall." But the way the chips fall has a degree of predictability. If a penny tossed a hundred times always came up heads, we might suspect that the penny is not a fair (well-balanced) coin. The geometry of the coin tells us that when it is tossed many times, heads and tails are equally likely. But a cowrie shell or half–walnut shell is not so predictable. We might test a particular shell and find that in the long run it is likely to land with the opening up about three times out of five. But would the same fraction hold true for a differently shaped shell?

Games of chance originated with attempts to foretell the future. They have been played with coins and dice, with cowrie shells and halves of nut shells, with spinners and tops, and with specially marked sticks. Here I describe the walnut shell game of the Paiute Indians, now living in northwestern Nevada. Similar games are common to many other Native American groups, as well as to peoples in other parts of the world.

Some parents may object to games that relate to gambling. Perhaps removing the words *win* and *lose* while discussing different outcomes can help to overcome their objections. Students and parents should be aware of the importance of probability in modern life. As just one example, the insurance industry is based entirely on theories of probability.

Walnut shell game (from Krause 1983)

Two or more children play. Each group of students will need eight walnut shell halves filled with clay and leveled off, a flat basket or bowl, and a quantity of toothpicks or small twigs to keep score.

How to play. Players take turns. Each player places the shells in the basket and tosses them. If three or five shells land with the flat (clay) side up, the player scores one point. No other combination wins points. Each player keeps count of his or her score with the small sticks.

To finish. Decide in advance how many rounds to play. The player with the highest score is the winner.

Discussion and Activities

• How likely is a walnut shell to land with the flat side up? Each student might toss one shell twenty times and record the number of times it lands with the flat side up. Then students can compare their outcomes. Compute the group averages and the class averages.

• Carry out the same experiment with coins.

• Is the walnut shell game a fair game or not? Explain.

• Play a similar game with cowrie shells or macaroni shells. Such a game, with four shells, is popular in many regions of Africa. The players note the number of shells that fall with openings up. The Igbo people of southeastern Nigeria call it igba-ita. Winning outcomes are all four up, all four down, or two up and two down. Students can discuss a scoring system.

• Play a game with a top, such as the *dreidel* used in December for the Jewish holiday Hanukkah.

NETWORKS

Background

Networks are an aspect of the field of mathematics called graph theory (not to be confused with algebraic or statistical graphs). Graph theory guides the setting up of telephone systems and TV networks. A genealogy tree is another example, as is the route of a traveling salesman. Basically, graph theory deals with points and the lines that connect them. The points might be cities and the lines would be the routes that lead from one to another.

Early in the twentieth century an anthropologist, Emil Torday, visited the region of the Kuba (or Bakuba) people of Zaire. One day he met several children kneeling in the sand and drawing intricate figures. They challenged him to copy these figures without lifting his finger or going over any segment of a line more than once. These are called *traceable networks*. In his book he wrote that the task was impossible! Yet these African children had carried it out.

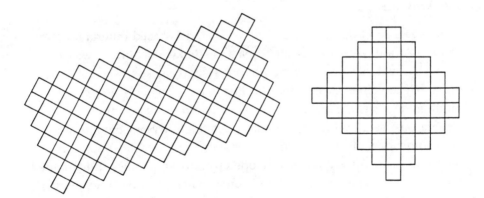

The Chokwe (Tchokwe, Tshokwe) of Angola have a tradition of drawing figures, called *sona* (singular *lusona*), in the sand to illustrate fables, riddles, history, and tales of morality. First the storyteller, always a man, constructs a grid of dots. Then he draws a figure, weaving between the dots as he tells his story. Many of these figures are drawn in one continuous line that returns to the starting point.

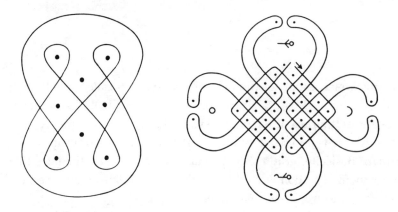

A network consists of a set of points (vertices) and the paths (arcs) connecting them. Two types of networks are *traceable*: (1) all the vertices are even—that is, an even number of arcs meet at each vertex—and you finish at the starting point; (2) exactly two vertices are odd and the others are even; start at one odd vertex and finish at the other.

Discussion and Activities

Many years ago I developed curriculum materials based on graph theory and the African networks of the Kuba and Chokwe peoples. I was able to test the materials over a period of one to two weeks in several sixth-grade self-contained classrooms and in a heterogeneously grouped ninth-grade social studies class. I purposely did not use a ninth-grade algebra class as a testing site because I wanted to try out the materials with students of all ability levels. After showing slides illustrating the wealth of mathematical ideas developed by African peoples, I distributed materials with suggestions for hands-on activities. At first three ninth graders rejected the materials—the instructors said they had done nothing but occupy space in class—but when they saw the other students engaged in animated discussion, they also wanted to participate. Obviously everyone was having fun!

Among the tasks I set were:

- Trace the network in one sweep of your pencil (the task that Torday declared impossible). I had included several nontraceable examples.

- For each *traceable* network, do you return to the starting point? Can you start anywhere, or must you start at a specific point?
- Continue the growth pattern for the Kuba network.

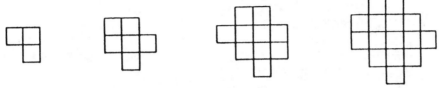

- Draw the traceable networks on grid paper.
- Can you decide about traceability without having actually to trace the network? [Some ninth graders were able to deduce the conditions.]

There was no question that the students enjoyed and were challenged by these materials. Their age seemed to have little bearing on their ability to follow through. One high school senior decided that as her term project she would teach the subject to a class of eighth graders, and she was chagrined to discover that some of her students did better than she. Sixth graders produced large colorful networks to decorate the walls of the classroom. Some were intrigued by the Chokwe myth that accompanied one design, and did further research on myths in general.

Milliken University instructor James Rauff used similar materials with eighth- and ninth-grade African Americans in a summer enrichment program (Rauff 1994). One day he looked out the window and commented about the amount of snow to be shoveled in the coming winter. A student said that it was just like the tracings they had done. Another added that you don't have to shovel all the paths, just enough to go from one building to another. Soon the whole class was drawing maps and making conjectures about minimal paths. "It was a beautiful, stimulating discussion on some real mathematics that the students had discovered a need for without any direction on my part" (3–4).

Chapter 12

Multicultural Mathematics Education in Practice

What Is Ideal Multicultural Mathematics Education?

Dr. Carl A. Grant, professor at the University of Wisconsin at Madison, is currently president of the National Association for Multicultural Education (NAME). In his article "Challenging the Myths About Multicultural Education" (1994), Grant exposes six common myths about multicultural education and provides the reader with facts to counter these myths.

Grant considers multicultural education a "philosophical concept and an educational process" (4). Both aspects are essential. One must be guided by the "philosophical ideals of freedom, justice, equality, equity, and human dignity" (4). He warns that equal access to the advantages that society can offer is not necessarily a guarantee of fairness in outcomes. For example, mandating that all students take algebra in ninth grade, without providing for those students who may not have been adequately prepared in the previous grades, may lead to an increase in the rate of dropouts rather than to a higher level of mathematical understanding for all students.

Grant stresses that multicultural education is a process that permeates "all academic disciplines and other aspects of the curriculum. It prepares all students to work actively toward structural equality in the organizations and institutions of the United States" (4). Mathematics, as well as other subjects, must deal realistically with the problems that students and their communities encounter in their lives, particularly with those factors that prevent the attainment of full equality.

Multicultural education "helps students to develop positive self-concepts and to discover who they are . . . by providing knowledge about the history, culture, and contributions of the diverse groups that have shaped the history, politics, and culture of the United States" (4). The preceding chapters of this book suggest many applications to mathematics.

Grant stresses the need for "a school staff that is multiracial and multiculturally literate. . . . [Multicultural education] confronts and seeks to bring about change of current social issues . . . by providing instruction in a context that students are familiar with, and builds upon students' diverse learning styles. It teaches critical-thinking skills, as well as democratic decision making, social action, and empowerment skills" (5).

He concludes his definition with the statement: "Multicultural education is a total process" (5).

How Can We Approach This Ideal?

An ideal teaching situation demands at least the following conditions:

- Well-developed curriculum materials that challenge all students both in mathematics and in related subject areas and that form an integral part of the total school curriculum.
- Support on the part of the school administration and faculty and of the community; opportunity for teams of teachers to plan jointly and evaluate the outcomes and to work with parents and the community.
- Heterogeneous classes; cooperative learning groups as appropriate; elimination of grouping by "ability"; student responsibility for their own learning.
- Assessment instruments that are aligned with the goals of multicultural mathematics education, to replace standardized multiple-choice tests.
- Professional development programs that educate teachers to fulfill the goals of multicultural mathematics education.

Basically, these ingredients are only slightly different from the requirements of the two reform movements—to restructure schools and to revise the teaching of mathematics at all levels. Those fortunate teachers and schools that have successfully navigated school restructuring and math curriculum reform now have the task of revising the curriculum to make their program multicultural.

At present I can cite no textbooks or complete programs for multicultural mathematics education at any level. I hope the situation will have changed for the better by the time you read this! The resources lists include some of the materials that are now available. You might incorporate these materials into a regular mathematics program and then proceed to build a curriculum using the suggestions in the preceding chapters of this book.

Realistically, I cannot conceive of any textbook or program that is entirely appropriate for all sectors of the population. Each school and each classroom teacher should tailor the curriculum to the needs of the students. He or she must answer such questions as:

- Should I stress the history, culture, and contributions of a specific racial/ethnic group, or should the approach be broader?
- What are the important issues in this community, and how do I incorporate them into the curriculum?
- To what extent do I focus on exposing and overcoming the injustices of society, such as racism, sexism, and poverty?

What advice can I give the teacher who is eager to multiculturalize the mathematics curriculum but has little support in the school? Go slow! Do the best you can. By involving the students and the community, you can at the same time enrich the curriculum and relieve yourself of some of the burdens of planning. As you proceed, try to involve other teachers. Be sensitive to the needs of all the students and be aware of the possible pitfalls.

What Do We Need to Watch Out For?

Sensitivity to all cultures
A participant in a course on multicultural mathematics education for teachers chose the topic of Gematria for her term paper (see page 86). In this system, letters of the alphabet are assigned numerical values and the sums of the values in a word or name are believed to have certain kinds of significance. She commented that she considered this practice to be part of her Jewish heritage, while she might label similar practices

in other cultures as pure superstition. She was well aware of her cultural biases!

Among the earliest groups that have lived longest in the Americas are the Native Peoples and the Africans who were brought to the New World in chains. These two groups are still the most oppressed in our society and have been the prime victims of stereotypical portrayals and misrepresentation in children's literature and educational materials, not to mention television and film.

Native Americans (some prefer to be called American Indians) are treated as though they are all the same, in spite of the fact that they once spoke hundreds of languages, some, unfortunately, now forgotten. In the past they lived in various types of houses, dressed differently from one another, and had varied lifestyles. Today many Native American groups own their own lands and consider themselves nations within the United States. Some indigenous Americans live in urban areas and are indistinguishable from their neighbors in their way of life, while others live on reservations. Whenever possible, the specific ethnic group or groups should be named, preferably by the names they use for themselves—Cherokee, Lakota, Diné, and so forth—rather than those given them by Europeans. Incidentally, Native American ancestry is part of the heritage of many people who consider themselves African American, Caribbean, or Mexican.

All students should be made aware of the scientific achievements of American Indians and of their respect for the land and all forms of life. At a 1989 conference, "Making Math Work for Minorities," Norbert Hill, Executive Director of the American Indian Sciences and Engineering Society (AISES), spoke of the over two hundred medicines in modern pharmacology, the solar-powered apartments at Mesa Verde, the five hundred miles of irrigation systems north of Phoenix built over two thousand years ago, and the Mesoamerican invention of the concept of zero. He might have added the invention of calendars and discoveries in astronomy; both require mathematical knowledge. Today the indigenous peoples of the world are teaching environmentalists about the preservation of our planet.

The continent of Africa, too, with its hundreds of diverse cultures, is often treated as though its peoples are all alike. A series of children's counting books has separate volumes for Mexico, Israel, and other countries, but just one volume for all of Africa. The number words are in Swahili, a language spoken in East Africa but unfamiliar to the majority of Africans.

Descriptive language

"A blend of exotic cultures and practical math concepts" was the catalog description of my book *Count on Your Fingers African Style* at the time it was published in 1980. What impression does the word *exotic* create? Doesn't it invoke images of peculiar customs of "strange" or even "primitive" African peoples? Would the word *exotic* have been used about the French style of finger counting?

In 1992 the National Broadcasting Corporation featured a week of programs describing the travels in Africa of its correspondents Bryant Gumbel and Katie Couric. In an interview, Gumbel said he hoped these programs would counter the "terrible images" most Americans have of Africa. "Africa is a land of two thousand languages and great religious diversity. . . . Americans view Africa as this monolithic land, as if it were France." He went on to admit to his own insensitivity. "We were going to do a piece about the vanishing tribes of Africa. A young African asked me why we can talk about the struggle in Yugoslavia between ethnic cultures, and when we come to Africa we call them tribes" (*New York Times* 1992, C12).

An African ethnic group numbering millions or tens of millions is often called a *tribe*, a denigrating term that would not be applied to a much smaller European population. Africans are said to live in *huts*, rather than in houses or dwellings. Authors often use the word *dialect* in referring to an African language, as though Africans are incapable of developing genuine languages. As a matter of fact, many Africans can speak at least one European language in addition to two or more African languages. Watch out for these buzz words, and many others. If you are not sure, apply the word to your own or a European culture to see how it fits.

The American population of African heritage has used a variety of terms to name themselves: colored, Negro, black, Black, Afro-American, African American. Although at any one time certain names are preferred, the others live on in the names of organizations: National Association for the Advancement of Colored People (NAACP), National Negro Women's Council, Congressional Black Caucus.

The United States Census Bureau lists Hispanics twice; they are included in the main categories of "black" or "white" depending on how they identify themselves, and again in a separate category for Hispanics. Many people of Spanish American heritage prefer to be considered Latino or Latina; those of Mexican ancestry often call themselves Chicano or Chicana.

White people are also the subject of various designations—white, White, Anglo, Caucasian, European American, to name a few. However, they are less likely than Africans or Native Peoples to be lumped all together. For instance, it is generally recognized that the original language, customs, and heritage of Irish Americans are quite different from those of Russian Americans.

Multiple perspectives on customs, practices, and worldview
First I'll tell you about a mistake I made through ignorance. In my activities book *Math Comes Alive* (1987) I had a lesson on symmetry in the masks of several cultures. To show lack of symmetry, I included an asymmetrical "false face" mask of the Haudenosaunee (Iroquois), copied from the Dover publication *American Indian Design and Decoration*, by LeRoy Appleton. At the time I did not realize that this mask was considered sacred. Some time later I had occasion to correspond with the Board of Education at the Akwesasne Mohawk School District in northern New York and southern Ontario. (The Mohawks are one of the six nations of the Iroquois Confederacy.) To ascertain that this use of the mask was not offensive, I sent a copy of the lesson to the Board's office. The reply confirmed my worst fears. Fortunately my book was due to undergo a major revision, and this lesson on masks was withdrawn from the new edition, *Multicultural Mathematics: Interdisciplinary Cooperative-Learning Activities* (1993a).

The following example refers to the contrast between European and American Indian perspectives. Mathematics teachers, particularly in New York City, often pose this question to their students:

> In 1626 the Dutch purchased the island of Manhattan for the equivalent of $24. If the Indians had invested this sum at six percent interest compounded annually, what would the investment be worth today? [Answer: more than $50 billion!]

This is a good opportunity to discuss with students the attitude of the Indians toward the land, in contrast to that of the Dutch and other Europeans. Indigenous people did not conceive of land as a commodity to be bought and sold. Land was a resource to be shared. When they accepted beads and other gifts from Europeans, they had no intention of giving away their Mother Earth in exchange.

Teachers must be mindful of the danger that students will judge societies by their degree of technological advancement and conclude that our society is superior. People all over the world and in all eras of history have engaged in mathematical activities to the extent of their needs and interests. A hunting and gathering society has no need for large numbers, while a society that engages in extensive trade must develop a consistent numeration system. When people are responsible for constructing their own homes, they devise the most practical techniques, depending on the available materials, the climate, and similar factors. Members of a community use the technology that is available to them until it no longer serves the purpose; then new methods are sought. Furthermore, students should realize the extent to which the industrialized Western nations depended on slavery and on domestic and colonial exploitation to attain their present wealth and advanced technology. At the same time, they should not be made to feel personally responsible for these acts; very likely their ancestors were also among the exploited.

In "Taking Multicultural, Anti-Racist Education Seriously" (Bigelow et al. 1994, 19–22) the Canadian educator Enid Lee responds to the question, How can one teach multiculturally without making white children feel guilty or threatened?

> First of all, recognize that there have always been white people who have fought against racism and social injustice. White children can proudly identify with these people and join in that tradition of fighting for social justice.
>
> Second, it is in their interest to be opening their minds and finding out how things really are. Otherwise, they will constantly have an incomplete picture of the human family.
>
> The other thing is, if we don't make it clear that some people benefit from racism, then we are being dishonest. What we have to do is talk about how young people can use that from which they benefit to change the order of things so that more people will benefit.(21)

Publishers can make mistakes, too. In their haste to jump on the multicultural bandwagon, some publishers have put on the market materials that had not been researched adequately, and in some cases were mathematically incorrect. In Chapter 5 I discuss errors in a lesson on the Igbo (Nigeria) system of number words. In response to the question in the Teachers' Guide as to how the Igbo name for 21 [sic] differs from our name for 21, the suggested answer is: "The Igbo system uses words; we use numbers." The authors made no distinction between spoken number words and written numerals. The impression given the children is that Africans were not capable of inventing written numerals. The fact is that the Igbo adopted the Indo-Arabic system when they found a need for it, just as Europeans did. In answer to my letter to the publisher pointing out the distinction between systems of number words and the Indo-Arabic system of symbols for numbers, an editor defended the lesson by stating that they don't like to use the word *numeral* with young children. She had missed the point entirely! Generally my experience with publishers has been more positive. They know that they might make errors and are grateful for corrections.

Sensitivity to students

Expectations. The level of performance that we expect of our students is often just what we get. The mathematical physicist, architect, and engineer Dr. Mario Salvadori, founder of the Salvadori Center on the Built Environment (see resources listings), tells how he teaches with math and science to "at risk" middle school students, those who are considered most likely to drop out long before they have completed high school. The key is to let students discover such concepts as weight, gravity, and leverage by working together on model building projects. Afterward they discuss the theoretical principles. This kind of hands-on learning leads to improvement in all subjects, not just math and science. Most important, students are motivated to do more. Mentors from the Center are impressed by how aware many young people in the program are of the problems in their own communities and by their ideas for solving these problems by designing good housing, community centers, health clinics, and similar facilities.

Sexism. Are girls and boys treated differently in the classroom? Do the girls have the opportunity to speak up as often as the boys? Research has shown that girls are likely to be evaluated on the basis of neatness and good behavior, while aggressive behavior in boys is accepted and even encouraged. Boys are expected to answer questions requiring higher-level thinking skills, in contrast to the purely factual questions addressed to girls.

Language facility and cultural background. Students who have inadequate facility with "standard" English may be considered incapable of using critical thinking skills in mathematics. Often such children are placed in low-level classes or groups, regardless of their achievement in mathematics.

Don't expect that children from a certain culture are familiar with the practices of that culture. They may not know them, or they may be shy about sharing their knowledge with the class. They may consider these customs old-fashioned or not like American ways. Teachers need to be aware of these possibilities.

Learning styles. Children with different personalities and cultural backgrounds are assigned to one classroom. Not only must they work together harmoniously but they must adapt to the instructional style of the teacher. Teachers should use a variety of visual, oral, and tactile approaches to accommodate students' learning styles. Furthermore, to quote University of Massachusetts professor Sonia Nieto in *Affirming Diversity* (1992):

> Most schools favor a highly competitive and individualistic
> instructional mode. In this kind of environment, dominant-
> culture children and males are more likely to succeed, whereas
> students from other cultural groups and females may be at a
> distinct disadvantage. By combining this style with a more
> cooperative mode, the learning and cultural styles of all
> children can be respected and valued. (119)

Last Words

I have proposed a broad and inclusive vision of multicultural mathematics education. Some people will disagree as to how, or even whether, to introduce such perspectives into the mathematics curriculum. According to University of Washington professor James A. Banks, our national salvation depends on the ideals and practices incorporated in a multicultural vision for our country. In his article

"Multicultural Education: Development, Dimensions, and Challenges" (1993) he writes:

> Most multiculturalists agree that the major goal of multicultural education is to restructure schools so that all students will acquire the knowledge, attitudes, and skills needed to function in an ethnically and racially diverse nation and world. As is the case with other interdisciplinary areas of study, debates within the field continue. These debates are consistent with the philosophy of a field that values democracy and diversity. They are also a source of strength. . . .
>
> The American identity is being reshaped, as groups on the margins of society begin to participate in the mainstream and to demand that their visions be reflected in a transformed America. In the future, the sharing of power and the transformation of identity required to achieve lasting racial peace in America may be valued rather than feared, for only in this way will we have national salvation. (27–28)

Resources

Children's Literature

Each children's book is listed under only one category, determined by the main theme of the book, although the book may deal with more than one mathematical topic. These lists are by no means exhaustive. New and wonderful books are always being published, and out-of-print books may be found in libraries. For further information about many of these books and suggestions about how they may be used in the classroom, see The Mathematics-Literature Connection listing.

Numbers

Birch, D. 1988. *The King's Chessboard*. New York: Dial. Growth by doubling, in an old tale from India, China, and Persia.

Carona, P. 1982. *Numbers*. Chicago: Childrens Press. Ancient numeration systems for young children.

Feelings, M. 1971. *Moja Means One: Swahili Counting Book*. New York: Dial.

Fisher, L. E. 1982. *Number Art: Thirteen 1 2 3s from Around the World*. New York: Four Winds.

Haskins, J. *Count Your Way Through [Various Countries]* Minneapolis: Carolrhoda. Series of books describing the counting words and cultures of many lands.

Hogben, L. 1968. *The Wonderful World of Numbers*. New York: Doubleday.

Lumpkin, B. 1992. *Senefer: A Young Genius in Old Egypt*. Lawrenceville, NJ: Africa World Press. Ancient Egyptian math in the context of an exciting story based on real life in ancient Egypt.

Moss, C. 1988. *Science in Ancient Mesopotamia*. New York: Franklin Watts.

Pittman, H. C. 1986. *A Grain of Rice*. New York: Hastings House. Based on the same folktale as *The King's Chessboard* (Birch 1988).

St. John, G. 1975. *How to Count Like a Martian.* New York: Walck. A mystery story about ancient and modern written systems of numeration.

Sitomer, M. & H. Sitomer. 1976. *How Did Numbers Begin?* New York: Crowell.

Trout, L. H. 1991. *The Maya.* New York: Chelsea House. Includes their numeration system and calendars.

Wahl, J. and S. Wahl. 1976. *I Can Count the Petals of a Flower.* Reston, VA: National Council of Teachers of Mathematics. Number names from one to sixteen in French, German, Italian, Spanish, and Hebrew; also includes the Hindi numerals.

Woods, G. 1988. *Science in Ancient Egypt.* New York: Franklin Watts.

Zaslavsky, C. 1980. *Count on Your Fingers African Style.* New York: Crowell. Reprinted 1996. New York: Black Butterfly. Counting and cultural background in Africa—East, West, and South.

———. 1989. *Zero: Is It Something? Is It Nothing?* New York: Franklin Watts.

Applications of Numbers

Adler, D. 1984. *All Kinds of Money.* New York: Franklin Watts.

Adler, I. & R. Adler. 1967. *The Calendar.* New York: John Day.

Anno, M. 1986. *All in a Day.* New York: Philomel.

———. 1987. *Anno's Sundial.* New York: Philomel.

Apfel, N. H. 1985. *Calendars.* New York: Franklin Watts.

Ashabranner, M. & B. Ashabranner. 1989. *Counting America: The Study of the United States Census.* New York: Putnam.

Beshore, G. 1988. *Science in Early Islamic Culture.* New York: Franklin Watts.

———. 1988. *Science in Ancient China.* New York: Franklin Watts.

Briers, A. 1987. *Money.* New York: Franklin Watts.

Bruchac, J. & J. London. 1992. *Thirteen Moons on Turtle's Back: A Native American Year of Moons.* New York: Philomel. Native American thirteen-month calendar and associated legends.

Burns, M. 1978. *This Book Is About Time.* Boston: Little, Brown.

Cantwell, L. 1984. *Money and Banking.* New York: Franklin Watts. For older students.

Cribb, J. 1990. *Money.* Eyewitness Books. New York: Knopf.

Dilson, J. 1968. *The Abacus: A Pocket Computer.* New York: St. Martin's Press.

Elkin, B. 1983. *Money.* Chicago: Childrens Press. Highly recommended.

Fisher, L. E. 1987. *Calendar Art: Thirteen Days, Weeks, Months, Years, from Around the World.* New York: Four Winds.

Leaf, M. 1987. *Eyes of the Dragon.* New York: Lothrop, Lee & Shepard. Introduces the Chinese abacus in a story for young children.

Maestro, B. 1993. *The Story of Money.* New York: Clarion. Good historically.

Migutch, A. 1985. *From Gold to Money.* Minneapolis: Carolrhoda.

Myller, R. 1991. *How Big Is a Foot?* New York: Dell.

Perry, S. 1981. *How Did We Get Clocks and Calendars?* Mankato, MN: Creative Education.

UNICEF. *The Little Cooks.* Cookbook. New York: U.S. Committee for UNICEF. To order: (800) 553-1200.

Yen, Clara. 1991. *Why Rat Comes First: The Story of the Chinese Zodiac.* Emeryville, CA: Children's Book Press.

Geometry in Art and Architecture

Blood, C. A. & M. Link. 1984. *Geraldine: The Goat in the Rug.* New York: Four Winds. Geraldine, the goat, tells about weaving a Navajo rug.

Campbell, M. 1992. *People of the Buffalo: How the Plains Indians Lived.* Buffalo, NY: Firefly Books, Ltd.

Coerr, E. 1977. *Sadako and the Thousand Paper Cranes.* New York: Putnam. Origami in the context of a true story about a Japanese girl dying of leukemia brought on by radiation from the atomic bomb.

Corwin, J. H. 1990. *African Crafts.* New York: Franklin Watts.

Erdoes, R. 1983. *The Native Americans.* Series. New York: Sterling.

Flournoy, V. 1985. *The Patchwork Quilt.* New York: Dutton.

Graymont, B. 1988. *The Iroquois.* New York: Chelsea House.

Grifalconi, A. 1987. *The Village of Round and Square Houses.* Boston: Little, Brown. Set in a village in Cameroon. Film based on the book: 1989. Weston, CT: Weston Woods Studio.

Hopkinson, D. 1993. *Sweet Clara and the Freedom Quilt.* New York: Knopf.

Hunt, W. B. 1954. *Indian Crafts and Lore.* New York: Golden Press. Patterns and instructions for beadwork, tipis, and decorative arts.

Isaacson, P. M. 1988. *Round Buildings, Square Buildings, and Buildings That Wiggle Like a Fish*. New York: Knopf.

Lavine, S. A. 1975. *The Houses the Indians Built*. New York: Dodd Mead.

Macaulay, D. A number of books about architecture for young people.

Morris, A. 1992. *Houses and Homes*. New York: Lothrop, Lee & Shepard.

Ridington, R. & J. Ridington. 1992. *People of the Longhouse: How the Iroquois Lived*. Buffalo, NY: Firefly Books Ltd.

Sarasas, C. 1964. *The ABCs of Origami: Paper-folding for Children*. Rutland, VT: Charles E. Tuttle.

Siska, H. S. *People of the Ice: How the Inuit Lived*. Buffalo, NY: Firefly Books Ltd.

Sitomer, M. & H. Sitomer. 1970. *What Is Symmetry?* New York: Crowell.

Steptoe, J. 1987. *Mufaro's Beautiful Daughters: An African Tale*. New York: Lothrop, Lee & Shepard. Illustrations inspired by ancient Zimbabwe.

Tompert, A. 1990. *Grandfather Tang's Story*. New York: Crown. Tangram story for young children.

Yue, C. & D. Yue. 1984. *The Tipi*. Boston: Houghton Mifflin.

———. 1986. *The Pueblo*. Boston: Houghton Mifflin.

———. 1988. *The Igloo*. Boston: Houghton Mifflin.

Community and Environment

There is a plethora of books on recycling, environmental concerns, and community action. Here are just a few.

Bowden, J. 1992. *Where Does Our Garbage Go?* New York: Doubleday.

Earthworks Group. 1990. *50 Simple Things Kids Can Do to Save the Earth*. Kansas City, MO: Andrews & McMeel.

Foster, J. 1991. *Cartons, Cans, and Orange Peels*. New York: Clarion.

Lewis, B. A. 1991. *The Kid's Guide to Social Action*. Minneapolis: Free Spirit.

Mendez, P. 1989. *The Black Snowman*. New York: Scholastic Hardcover.

Miles, B. 1991. *Save the Earth: An Action Handbook for Kids*. New York: Knopf.

Perl, Lila. 1994. *The Great Ancestor Hunt*. Boston: Houghton Mifflin. Techniques and resources to trace genealogy.

Wilcox, C. 1988. *Trash*. Minneapolis: Carolrhoda.

Games

Adler, I. 1974. *Magic House of Numbers*. New York: John Day.

Arnold, A. 1972. *The World of Children's Games*. New York: World Times Mirror.

Bell, R. & M. Cornelius. 1988. *Board Games Round the World*. New York: Cambridge University Press.

Blood, Charles. 1981. *American Indian Games and Crafts*. New York: Franklin Watts.

Grunfeld, F. V., ed. 1975. *Games of the World: How to Make Them, How to Play Them, How They Came to Be*. New York: Ballantine. A real treasury.

Orlando, L. 1993. *The Multicultural Game Book: More Than Seventy Traditional Games from Thirty Countries*. New York: Scholastic Professional.

Sackson, S. 1991. *The Book of Classic Board Games*. Palo Alto, CA: Klutz Press.

Zaslavsky, C. 1982. *Tic Tac Toe and Other Three-in-a-Row Games, from Ancient Egypt to the Modern Computer*. New York: Crowell. Includes cultural and historical background.

Biography

Few books for children describe the lives of mathematicians. However, mathematics is an important element in many fields of achievement—science, art, architecture, athletics, public service, social action, union organizing, to name just a few. The list below is a sampling of the available literature that might be tied in with topics in mathematics.

Billings, C. W. 1989. *Grace Hopper: Navy Admiral and Computer Pioneer*. Hillside, NJ: Enslow.

Conley, K. 1989. *Benjamin Banneker: Scientist and Mathematician*. New York: Chelsea House.

Davis, M. P. 1990. *Mexican Voices: American Dreams*. New York: Henry Holt. Artist Diego Rivera, among others.

Haber, L. 1970. *Black Pioneers of Science and Invention*. New York: Harcourt Brace.

Hayden, R. C. 1970. *Seven Black American Scientists*. Reading, MA: Addison-Wesley.

Lasky, K. 1994. *The Librarian Who Measured the Earth*. Boston: Little, Brown. About Eratosthenes, born in North Africa, educated in Athens, chief librarian of the university at Alexandria, Egypt.

Morey, J. N. & W. Dunn. 1992. *Famous Asian Americans*. New York: Cobblehill. Architect I. M. Pei, among others.

Otfinski, S. 1993. *Marian Wright Edelman: Defender of Children's Rights*. Woodbridge, CT: Blackbirch Press.

Perl, T. 1978. *Math Equals: Biographies of Women Mathematicians plus Related Activities*. Menlo Park, CA: Addison-Wesley.

———. 1993. *Women and Numbers: Lives of Women Mathematicians plus Discovery Activities*. San Carlos, CA: Wide World/Tetra. Includes contemporary women of varied ethnic/racial heritage.

Pinkney, Andrea Davis. 1994. *Dear Benjamin Banneker*. New York: Harcourt Brace.

Scheader, C. 1990. *Shirley Chisholm: Teacher and Congresswoman*. Hillside, NJ: Enslow.

Siegel, B. 1995. *Marian Wright Edelman: The Making of a Crusader*. New York: Simon & Schuster Books for Young Readers.

Stantrey, L. 1983. *Jim Thorpe: Young Athlete*. Mahwah, NJ: Troll.

White, F. M. 1973. *Cesar Chavez: Man of Courage*. New York: Dell.

The Mathematics-Literature Connection

The following references are not confined to multicultural literature, but can furnish additional information about many of the books listed in the previous section.

Kolakowski, J. S. 1992. *Linking Math with Literature*. Greensboro, NC: Carson-Dellosa.

Slapin, B. & D. Seale. 1992. *Through Indian Eyes: The Native Experience in Books for Children*. Philadelphia: New Society. Offers extremely useful guidelines for analyzing children's books for authenticity and possible stereotypes, but is not specifically about mathematics literature.

Thiessen, D. & M. Matthias. 1992. *The Wonderful World of Mathematics*. Reston, VA: National Council of Teachers of Mathematics.

Welchmans-Tischler, R. 1992. *How to Use Children's Literature to Teach Mathematics*. Reston, VA: National Council of Teachers of Mathematics.

Whitin, D. & S. Wilde. 1992. *Read Any Good Math Lately?* Portsmouth, NH: Heinemann.

———. 1995. *It's the Story That Counts*. Portsmouth, NH: Heinemann.

Multicultural Math Activities for Students

Curriculum Associates. 1994. *Kaleidoscope: Count On It!* North Billerica, MA: Curriculum Associates. Grades 3–5.

Education Development Center. *Seeing and Thinking Mathematically in the Middle Grades.* Series. Portsmouth, NH: Heinemann. Grades 6–8. Series includes:
1994. *The Language of Numbers.*
1994. *From the Ground Up: Modeling, Measuring, and Constructing Houses.*
1995. *Designing Spaces: Visualizing, Planning, and Building.*
1995. *Chance Encounters: Probability in Games and Simulations.*

Gilmer, G., M. Soniat-Thompson & C. Zaslavsky. 1992. *Building Bridges to Mathematics: Cultural Connections.* Menlo Park, CA: Addison-Wesley. Set of activity cards for each grade, K–8.

Irons, C. J., et al. 1994. *Mathematics from Many Cultures.* San Francisco: Mimosa. Posters, big book, and teacher's book for each grade, from kindergarten up.

Krause, M. 1983. *Multicultural Mathematics Materials.* Reston, VA: National Council of Teachers of Mathematics.

Lumpkin, B. & D. Strong. 1995. *Multicultural Science and Math Connections: Middle School Projects and Activities.* Portland, ME: J. Weston Walch.

Perl, T. See listings under Children's Literature: Biography.

Seattle Public Schools. 1984. *Multicultural Mathematics Posters and Activities.* Reston, VA: National Council of Teachers of Mathematics.

Swetz, F. J. 1993. *Learning Activities from the History of Mathematics.* Portland, ME: J. Weston Walch. Middle and secondary levels.

The two books below contain blackline masters for many of the activities that I have described in this book:

Zaslavsky, C. 1993. *Multicultural Mathematics: Interdisciplinary Cooperative-Learning Activities.* Portland, ME: J. Weston Walch. Grades 6 and up.

———. 1994. *Multicultural Math: Hands-On Activities from Around the World.* New York: Scholastic Professional. Grades 3–6.

Selected Articles from the *Arithmetic Teacher*

Binswinger, R. 1988. "Discovering Perimeter and Area with Logo." 36(September):18–24.

Bradley, C. 1992. "The Four Directions Indian Beadwork." 39(May):46–49.

————. 1993. "Making a Navajo Blanket Design with Logo." 40(May):520–23.

Campbell, P. F. & C. Langrall. 1993. "Making Equity a Reality in Classrooms." 41(October):110–13.

Carey, D. 1992. "The Patchwork Quilt: A Context for Problem Solving." 40(December):199–203.

Dorward, J. & S. Archibald. 1994. "Linking Teacher Interests or Backgrounds to Real World Experiences for Students." 41(February):300–303. Fifth-grade students built scale models of Indian habitats and a log cabin.

Giganti, P. & M. Cittadino. 1990. "The Art of Tessellations." 37(March):6–16.

Kaiser, B. 1988. "Explorations with Tessellating Polygons." 36(December):19–24.

Lambdin, D. V. & V. L. Walker. 1994. "Planning for Classroom Portfolio Assessment." 41(February):318–24.

Taylor, L., et al. 1991. "American Indians, Mathematical Attitudes, and the *Standards*." 38(February):14–21.

Whitin, D. J. 1993. "Looking at the World from a Mathematical Perspective." 40(April):438–41.

Zaslavsky, C. 1981. "Networks—New York Subways, a Piece of String, and African Traditions." 29(October):36–43.

————. 1989. "People Who Live in Round Houses." 37(September):18–21.

————. 1990. "Symmetry in American Folk Art." 38(September):6–12.

————. 1991. "Multicultural Mathematics Education for the Middle Grades." 38(February):8–13.

Zepp, R. A. 1992. "Numbers and Codes in Ancient Peru: The Quipu." 39(May):42–45. Note that the quipu is portrayed incorrectly.

Mathematics Education—General

California Department of Education. 1992. *Mathematics Framework for California Public Schools: Kindergarten Through Grade Twelve.* Sacramento: California Department of Education.

National Council of Teachers of Mathematics. 1989. *Curriculum and Evaluation Standards for School Mathematics.* Reston, VA: NCTM.

————. 1991. *Professional Standards for Teaching Mathematics.* Reston, VA: NCTM.

Ohanian, S. 1992. *Garbage Pizza, Patchwork Quilts, and Math Magic.* New York:

Freeman. Available through Heinemann, Portsmouth, NH. Emphasis on parental involvement and the culture of the community.

Parker, R. E. 1993. *Mathematical Power: Lessons from a Classroom.* Portsmouth, NH: Heinemann. Inspiring story of a year in a fifth-grade classroom as the author, the classroom teacher, and her students struggle together to bring the NCTM *Standards* to life. Practical experiences with planning, management of cooperative learning groups, and assessment.

Stenmark, J. K., ed. 1991. *Mathematics Assessment: Myths, Models, Good Questions, and Practical Suggestions.* Reston, VA: National Council of Teachers of Mathematics.

Stenmark, J. K., P. Beck & H. Asturias. 1994. "Assessment: A Room with More Than One View." *Mathematics Teaching in the Middle School* 1(1):44–49.

Multicultural Perspectives and Equity Issues—General Education

Allen, J., E. McNeil, & V. Schmidt. 1992. *Cultural Awareness for Children* (Grades K–3). Menlo Park, CA: Addison-Wesley. Includes number words in eight languages, several from Asia.

Anyon, J. 1980. "Social Class and the Hidden Curriculum of Work." *Journal of Education* 162(Winter):67–92.

Asante, M. K. 1991–1992. "Afrocentric Curriculum." *Educational Leadership* 49(4):28–31. Entire issue is entitled *Whose Culture?*

Atwater, M. M., K. Radzik-Marsh & M. Strutchens, eds. 1994. *Multicultural Education: Inclusion of All.* Athens, GA: University of Georgia Press.

Baker, G. C. 1994. *Planning and Organizing for Multicultural Instruction.* Second edition. Menlo Park, CA: Addison-Wesley.

Banks, J. A. 1993. "Multicultural Education: Development, Dimensions, and Challenges." *Phi Delta Kappan* 75(1):22–28. Special issue on multicultural education.

Banks, J. A. & C. A. McGee Banks, eds. 1995. *Handbook of Research on Multicultural Education.* New York: Macmillan. Over a thousand pages, written by the leading figures in the field.

Bigelow, B., et al., 1994. *Rethinking Our Classrooms: Teaching for Equity and Justice.* Milwaukee, WI: Rethinking Schools. (See "Other Resources.")

Davidman, L., with P. T. Davidman. 1994. *Teaching with a Multicultural Perspective: A Practical Guide.* White Plains, NY: Longman. The authors present an integrated model of multicultural curriculum and instruction, exemplified by interdisciplinary units on such topics as ancient Egypt, prevention of smoking, and the environment. Annotated lists of resources.

Grant, C. 1994. "Challenging the Myths About Multicultural Education." *Multicultural Education* 2(2):4–9.

Kohl, H. 1994. *"I Won't Learn from You" and Other Thoughts on Creative Maladjustment*. New York: New Press.

Ladson-Billings, G. 1994. *The Dreamkeepers: Successful Teachers of African American Children*. San Francisco: Jossey-Bass.

Nieto, S. 1992. *Affirming Diversity: The Sociopolitical Context of Multicultural Education*. New York: Longman.

Perry, T. & J. W. Fraser, eds. 1993. *Freedom's Plow: Teaching in the Multicultural Classroom*. New York: Routledge.

Multicultural Perspectives and Equity Issues—Mathematics Education

I have omitted the well-known and useful texts on the history of mathematics by Carl Boyer, Howard Eves, Edna Kramer, H. O. Midonick, David Eugene Smith, Dirk Struik, and others.

Ascher, M. 1991. *Ethnomathematics: A Multicultural View of Mathematical Ideas*. Belmont, CA: Brooks/Cole.

Ascher, M. & R. Ascher. 1980. *The Code of the Quipu*. Ann Arbor: University of Michigan Press.

Bedini, S. 1972. *The Life of Benjamin Banneker*. New York: Scribner's.

Bibliography of Multicultural Issues in Mathematics. 1994. Available through Dr. Patricia S. Wilson, Mathematics Education Department, University of Georgia, 105 Aderhold Hall, Athens, GA 30602.

Bishop, A. J. 1988. *Mathematical Enculturation: A Cultural Perspective on Mathematics Education*. Boston: Kluwer.

Clewell, B. C., B. T. Anderson & M. E. Thorpe. 1992. *Breaking the Barriers: Helping Female and Minority Students Succeed in Mathematics and Science*. San Francisco: Jossey-Bass.

Closs, M. P., ed. 1986. *Native American Mathematics*. Austin: University of Texas Press.

Cocking, R. R. & J. P. Mestre, eds. 1988. *Linguistic and Cultural Influences on Learning Mathematics*. Hillside, NJ: Erlbaum.

D'Ambrosio, U. 1985. "Ethnomathematics and Its Place in the History and Pedagogy of Mathematics." *For the Learning of Mathematics* 5(2):44–48.

Denyer, S. 1978. *African Traditional Architecture*. New York: Africana.

Fauvel, J. P. & P. Gerdes. 1990. "African Slave and Calculating Prodigy." *Historia Mathematica* 17(2):141–51. About Thomas Fuller (1710–1790).

Fennema, E. & G. C. Leder, eds. 1990. *Mathematics and Gender*. New York: Teachers College Press.

Gerdes, P. 1988. "On Culture, Geometric Thinking and Mathematics Education." *Educational Studies in Mathematics* 19(2):137–62.

Gillings, R. 1972. *Mathematics in the Time of the Pharaohs*. New York: Dover.

Grinstein, L. & P. Campbell, eds. 1987. *Women of Mathematics: A Bibliographic Sourcebook*. Westport, CT: Greenwood.

Harris, M. 1987. "An Example of Traditional Women's Work as a Mathematical Resource." *For the Learning of Mathematics* 7(3):26–28.

Heckman, P. E. & J. Weissglass. 1994. "Contextualized Mathematics Instruction: Moving Beyond Recent Proposals." *For the Learning of Mathematics* 14(1):29–33.

Ifrah, G. 1985. *From One to Zero: A Universal History of Numbers*. New York: Viking.

Joseph, G. G. 1991. *The Crest of the Peacock: Non-European Roots of Mathematics*. London: I. B. Tauris. 1992. New York: Penguin.

Journal of Negro Education 1990. 59(3). Entire issue on mathematics and science education.

Katz, V. 1993. *A History of Mathematics*. New York: HarperCollins.

Kenschaft, P. C. & S. Z. Keith, eds. 1991. *Winning Women into Mathematics*. Washington, DC: Mathematical Association of America.

Lipka, J. 1994. "Culturally Negotiated Schooling: Toward a Yup'ik Mathematics." *Journal of American Indian Education* 33(Spring):14–30.

Lipka, J. & T. L. McCarty. 1994. "Changing the Culture of Schooling: Navajo and Yup'ik Cases." *Anthropology & Education Quarterly* 25(3):266–84.

Lumpkin, B. 1989. "African and African-American Contributions to Mathematics." In *African-American Baseline Essays*. Ed. A. Hilliard & C. Leonard. Portland, OR: Portland Public Schools.

Menninger, K. 1992. *Number Words and Number Symbols*. Cambridge, MA: MIT Press, 1969. Reprint, New York: Dover.

Moses, R. P., et al. 1989. "The Algebra Project: Organizing in the Spirit of Ella." *Harvard Educational Review* 59(4):27–47.

Nelson, D., G. G. Joseph & J. Williams. 1993. *Multicultural Mathematics: Teaching Mathematics from a Global Perspective.* Oxford, UK: Oxford University Press.

Newell, V. K., et al., eds. 1980. *Black Mathematicians and Their Works.* Ardmore, PA: Dorrance.

Oakes, J. 1990. *Multiplying Inequalities: The Effects of Race, Social Class, and Tracking on Opportunities to Learn Mathematics and Science.* Santa Monica, CA: Rand Corporation.

Olivastro, D. 1993. *Ancient Puzzles.* New York: Bantam.

Pappas, Theoni. 1989. *The Joy of Mathematics.* San Carlos, CA: Wide World/Tetra.

Ratteray, J. D., et al. 1991. *Teaching Mathematics: African-Based Themes for the Classroom.* Washington, DC: Institute for Independent Education.

Rauff, J. V. 1994. "How Students Can Own Mathematics: Three Tales." *ISGEm Newsletter* 9(2):3–4 (See "Other Resources" for the address).

Russ, L. 1984. *Mancala Games.* Algonac, MI: Reference.

Salvadori, S. 1990. *The Art of Construction: Projects and Principles for Beginning Engineers and Architects.* Chicago: Chicago Review Press.

Schimmel, A. 1993. *The Mystery of Numbers.* New York: Oxford University Press.

Secada, W. G. 1994. "Towards a Consciously Multicultural Mathematics Curriculum." In *Reinventing Urban Education: Multiculturalism and Social Context in Schooling,* ed. F. L. Rivera-Batiz, 235–55. New York: IUME Press, Institute for Urban and Minority Education, Teachers College.

Secada, W. G., E. Fennema & L. B. Adajian, eds. 1995. *New Directions for Equity in Mathematics Education.* New York: Cambridge University Press. Also available from NCTM.

Secada, W. G. & M. Meyer, eds. 1989. "Needed: An Agenda for Equity in Mathematics Education." *Peabody Journal of Education* 66(2). Entire issue.

Shirley, L. (in press). "Activities from African Calendar and Time Customs." *Mathematics Teaching in the Middle School.*

Smith, Jacquelin. 1995. "Threading Mathematics into Social Studies." *Teaching Children Mathematics* 1(March):438–44.

Tate, W. F. 1994. "Race, Retrenchment, and the Reform of School Mathematics." *Phi Delta Kappan* 75(6):477–84.

Van Sertima, I., ed. 1983. *Blacks in Science, Ancient and Modern.* New Brunswick, NJ: Transaction Books.

Washburn, D. K. & D. W. Crowe. 1988. *Symmetries of Culture: Theory and Practice of Plane Pattern Analysis.* Seattle: University of Washington Press.

Zaslavsky, C. 1979. *Africa Counts: Number and Pattern in African Culture.* New York: Lawrence Hill Books.

————. 1983. "Essay Review" of Literature on African American Mathematicians. *Historia Mathematica* 10(2):105–15.

————. 1991. "World Cultures in the Mathematics Class." *For the Learning of Mathematics* 11(2):32–36.

————. 1993. "Multicultural Mathematics: One Road to the Goal of Mathematics for All." In *Reaching All Students with Mathematics,* ed. G. Cuevas & M. Driscoll, 45–55. Reston, VA: National Council of Teachers of Mathematics.

————. 1994. *Fear of Math: How to Get Over It and Get On with Your Life.* New Brunswick, NJ: Rutgers University Press. User-friendly analysis of the societal factors that induce fear of math, particularly among many females and people of color—stereotypes about who can do math, inferior schooling, low-level and poorly taught math curriculum—much of it told in the words of the victims. Demonstrates the importance of math for the citizen with vignettes about the use and misuse of math.

Other Resources: Organizations, Institutions, and Miscellaneous

Algebra Project. Director: Robert Moses. 99 Bishop Allen Drive, Cambridge, MA 02139, (617) 491-0200. Middle school students in low-income communities build on their life experiences to learn advanced mathematics.

Association for Supervision and Curriculum Development (ASCD). *Multicultural Education* program includes videotapes, facilitator's guide, and the invaluable book *Teaching with a Multicultural Perspective* (Davidman, 1994).

Children's Defense Fund. Director: Marian Wright Edelman, 25 E Street, NW, Washington, DC 20001, (202) 628-8787. Publishes annual *Stae of America's Children.*

Family Math. Director: Virginia Thompson, Lawrence Hall of Science, University of California, Berkeley, CA 94720, (510) 642-1823. Publishes *Family Math* book in several languages.

International Study Group on Ethnomathematics (ISGEm). President: Gloria Gilmer, Math-Tech, Inc., 9155 North 70th Street, Milwaukee, WI 53223.

International Study Group on the Relations Between History and Pedagogy of Mathematics (HPM). Newsletter editor: Victor J. Katz, Department of Mathematics, University of the District of Columbia, 4200 Connecticut Avenue, NW, Washington, DC 20008.

Metropolitan Museum of Art. Publishes *The Mathematics of Islamic Art*, a kit of slides and lessons. 1000 Fifth Avenue, New York, NY 10028, (212) 570-3723.

National Association for Multicultural Education (NAME). President: Carl A. Grant. Publishes journal, *Multicultural Education*. To subscribe: Caddo Gap Press, 3145 Geary Blvd., #275, San Francisco, CA 94118, (415) 750-9978.

National Council of Teachers of Mathematics, 1906 Association Drive, Reston, VA 22091-1593, (703) 620-9840.

National Women's History Project. Publishes annual catalog: 7738 Bell Road, Windsor, CA 95492, (707) 838-6000.

Portland (Oregon) Public Schools. Publishes *Baseline Essays Mathematics* for the following cultures: African American, American Indian, Asian-American, and Hispanic-American. (503) 331-3270.

Rethinking Schools, Ltd. Publishes *Rethinking Schools (An Urban Education Journal)* and other publications: 1001 E. Keefe Avenue, Milwaukee, WI 53212, (414) 964-9646.

Salvadori Educational Center on the Built Environment, City College of New York, Harris Hall, Room 202, 138th Street and Convent Avenue, New York, NY 10031, (212) 650-5497.

School Science and Mathematics Association, Department of Curriculum and Foundations, Bloomsburg University, 400 East Second Street, Bloomsburg, PA 17815-1301, (717) 389-4915.

UNICEF. Issues annual *State of the World's Children* (Oxford University Press).

U.S. Census Bureau Education Program (K–12). Data User Services Division, Department IM, Washington, DC 20233-8300, (301) 763-1510.

Women in Mathematics Education (WME). C/o SummerMath, 302 Shattuck Hall, Mt. Holyoke College, South Hadley, MA 01075, (413) 538-2608.

References

Anyon, J. 1980. "Social Class and the Hidden Curriculum of Work." *Journal of Education* 162 (Winter): 67–92.

Ascher, M. 1991. *Ethnomathematics: A Multicultural View of Mathematical Ideas.* Belmont, CA: Brooks/Cole.

Ascher, M., and R. Ascher. 1980. *The Code of the Quipu.* Ann Arbor: University of Michigan Press.

Ashabranner, M., and B. Ashabranner. 1989. *Counting America: The Study of the United States Census.* New York: Putnam.

Baker, G. C. 1994. *Planning and Organizing for Multicultural Instruction.* Second edition. Menlo Park, CA: Addison-Wesley.

Banks, J. A. 1993. "Multicultural Education: Development, Dimensions, and Challenges." *Phi Delta Kappan* 75(1): 22–28.

Barber, E. W. 1994. *Women's Work.* New York: Norton.

Bell, R., and M. Cornelius. 1988. *Board Games Around the World.* New York: Cambridge University Press.

Bigelow, B., et al., eds. 1994. *Rethinking Our Classrooms: Teaching for Equity and Justice.* Milwaukee, WI: Rethinking Schools. (See "Other Resources.")

Bruchac, J., and J. London. 1992. *Thirteen Moons on Turtle's Back.* New York: Philomel.

California Department of Education. 1992. *Mathematics Framework for California Public Schools: Kindergarten Through Grade Twelve.* Sacramento: California Department of Education.

Children's Defense Fund. *The State of America's Children.* Annual report. (See "Other Resources.")

Clark, R. 1983. *Family Life and School Achievement: Why Poor Black Children Succeed or Fail.* Chicago: University of Chicago Press.

Clinkscales, Gwendolyn. Personal communication.

Coerr, E. 1977. *Sadako and the Thousand Paper Cranes*. New York: Putnam.

Cohen, Grace. Personal communication.

Conley, K. 1989. *Benjamin Banneker: Scientist and Mathematician*. New York: Chelsea House.

Dailey, M. C., and E. D. Washington. 1985. "The Evolution of Doxey A. Wilkerson, 1935–1945." *Freedomways* 25(Summer): 101–115.

Davidman, L., with P. T. Davidman. 1994. *Teaching with a Multicultural Perspective: A Practical Guide*. White Plains, NY: Longman.

Denyer, S. 1978. *African Traditional Architecture*. New York: Africana.

Dryfoos, J. G. 1994. *Full Service Schools*. San Francisco: Jossey-Bass.

Earthworks Group. 1990. *50 Simple Things Kids Can Do to Save the Earth*. Kansas City, MO: Andrews & McMeel.

Education Development Center. 1994. *The Language of Numbers*. Portsmouth, NH: Heinemann.

FairTest Examiner. 1994. "Kentucky Eliminates Multiple Choice Questions." 8(Fall): 7.

Feelings, M. 1971. *Moja Means One*. New York: Dial.

Ferrucci, Beverly. Personal communication.

First Books: Science in Ancient Times series. 1988. New York: Franklin Watts.

Flournoy, V. 1985. *The Patchwork Quilt*. New York: Dutton.

Grant, C. 1994. "Challenging the Myths About Multicultural Education." *Multicultural Education* 2(2): 4–9.

Grifalconi, A. 1987. *The Village of Round and Square Houses*. Boston: Little, Brown.

Grossman, V. 1991. *Ten Little Rabbits*. San Francisco: Chronicle.

Haskins, J. 1989. *Count Your Way Through Africa*. Minneapolis: Carolrhoda.

Heckman, P. E., and J. Weissglass. 1994. "Contextualized Mathematics Instruction: Moving Beyond Recent Proposals." *For the Learning of Mathematics* 14(1): 29–33.

Hill, N. 1990. "The American Indian Sciences and Engineering Society." In *Making Mathematics Work for Minorities: A Compendium of Papers*, 96–99. Washington, DC: Mathematical Sciences Education Board.

Hopkinson, D. 1993. *Sweet Clara and the Freedom Quilt*. New York: Knopf.

Ifrah, G. 1985. *From One to Zero.* New York: Viking.

Ilutsik, Esther. Personal communication.

Jacobson, S. A. 1984. *Yup'ik Eskimo Dictionary.* Fairbanks, AK: Alaska Native Learning Center, University of Alaska.

Kohl, Herbert. 1994. *"I Won't Learn from You" and Other Thoughts on Creative Maladjustment.* New York: New Press.

Krause, M. 1983. *Multicultural Mathematics Materials.* Reston, VA: NCTM.

Ladson-Billings, G. 1994. *The Dreamkeepers.* San Francisco: Jossey-Bass.

———. 1995. "Making Mathematics Meaningful in Multicultural Contexts." In *New Directions for Equity in Mathematics Education,* Secada et al., eds., 126–45.

Lave, J. 1988. *Cognition in Practice.* New York: Cambridge University Press.

Lee, E. 1994. "Taking Multicultural Anti-Racist Education Seriously." In *Rethinking Our Classrooms,* Bigelow et al., eds., 19–22.

Lipka, J. 1994. "Culturally Negotiated Schooling: Toward a Yup'ik Mathematics." *Journal of American Indian Education* 33(Spring): 14–30.

Lumpkin, B. 1992. *A Young Genius in Old Egypt.* Lawrenceville, NJ: Africa World Press.

Maestro, B. 1993. *The Story of Money.* New York: Clarion.

Marshack, A. 1991. *The Roots of Civilization.* Mt. Kisco, NY: Moyer Bell.

McKnight, C. C. 1987. *The Underachieving Curriculum.* Champaign, IL: Stipes.

McShane, J. B. 1994. "Paper Profits." *New York Times* (February 12): OP-ED.

Mendez, P. 1989. *The Black Snowman.* New York: Scholastic Hardcover.

Morris, A. 1992. *Houses and Homes.* New York: Lothrop, Lee & Shepard.

Murray, C., & R. Herrnstein. 1994. *The Bell Curve.* New York: Free Press.

Myller, R. 1991. *How Big Is a Foot?* New York: Dell.

National Council of Teachers of Mathematics. 1989. *Curriculum and Evaluation Standards for School Mathematics.* Reston, VA: NCTM.

Neihardt, J. G. 1961. *Black Elk Speaks.* Lincoln: University of Nebraska Press.

Ohanian, S. 1992. *Garbage Pizza, Patchwork Quilts, and Math Magic.* New York: Freeman.

Otfinski, S. 1993. *Marian Wright Edelman: Defender of Children's Rights.* Woodbridge, CT: Blackbirch Press.

Parker, R. 1993. *Mathematical Power*. Portsmouth, NH: Heinemann.

Perl, Lila. 1994. *The Great Ancestor Hunt*. Boston: Houghton Mifflin.

Perl, Teri. 1993. *Women and Numbers*. San Carlos, CA: Wide World/Tetra.

Perry, T., and J. W. Fraser, eds. 1993. *Freedom's Plow*. New York: Routledge.

Rauff, J. V. 1994. "How Students Can Own Mathematics: Three Tales." *ISGEm Newsletter* 9(2): 3–4. (See "Other Resources" for the address.)

Richards, J. J. 1993. "Classroom Tapestry: A Practitioner's Perspective on Multicultural Education." In *Freedom's Plow*, edited by Perry and Fraser, 47–89.

Richardson, L. 1994. "Teacher Advising Education Chief Draws Lessons from Own History." *New York Times* (November 23): B8.

Sarasas, C. 1964. *The ABCs of Origami*. Rutland, VT: Charles E. Tuttle.

Schimmel, A. 1993. *The Mystery of Numbers*. New York: Oxford University Press.

Schubeck, Kathryn. Personal communication.

Secada, W. G. 1994. "Towards a Consciously-Multicultural Mathematics Curriculum." In *Reinventing Urban Education: Multiculturalism and Social Context in Schooling*, edited by F. L. Rivera-Batiz, 235–55. New York: IUME Press, Institute for Urban and Minority Education, Teachers College.

Secada, W. G., E. Fennema, and L. B. Adajian, eds. 1995. *New Directions for Equity in Mathematics Education*. New York: Cambridge University Press.

Shirley, Lawrence. Personal communication.

Siegel, Beatrice. 1995. *Marian Wright Edelman: The Making of a Crusader*. New York: Simon & Schuster Books for Young Readers.

Sizer, T. 1984. *Horace's Compromise*. Boston: Houghton Mifflin.

Slapin, B., & D. Seale. 1992. *Through Indian Eyes: The Native Experience in Books for Children*. Philadelphia: New Society.

Smith, J. 1995. "Threading Mathematics into Social Studies." *Teaching Children Mathematics*. 1(March): 438–44.

Steptoe, J. 1987. *Mufaro's Beautiful Daughters*. New York: Lothrop, Lee & Shepard.

Strutchens, Marilyn. Personal communication.

Tate, W. F. 1994. "Race, Retrenchment, and the Reform of School Mathematics." *Phi Delta Kappan* 75(6): 477–84.

Technology Applications Quarterly. 1994. "Update: The Luis Muñoz Marin School." 5(Spring): 23. Albany: New York State Education Department.

"Tobacco Industry Seeks New Recruits." 1993. *American Educator* 17(Spring): 42.

Tompert, A. 1990. *Grandfather Tang's Story.* New York: Crown.

UNICEF. 1994. *The State of the World's Children.* Annual report. New York: Oxford University Press.

Whitin, D. J. 1992. Review of *Ten Little Rabbits. Arithmetic Teacher* 39(September): 56–57.

———. 1993. Response to letter to the editor. *Arithmetic Teacher* 41(October): 114–15.

Whitin, D. J., and S. Wilde. 1992. *Read Any Good Math Lately?* Portsmouth, NH: Heinemann.

———. 1995. *It's the Story That Counts.* Portsmouth, NH: Heinemann.

Woods, G. 1988. *Science in Ancient Egypt.* New York: Franklin Watts.

Zaslavsky, C. 1979. *Africa Counts.* New York: Lawrence Hill Books.

———. 1980. *Count on Your Fingers African Style.* New York: Crowell. Reprinted 1996. New York: Black Butterfly.

———. 1989. "People Who Live in Round Houses." *Arithmetic Teacher* 37(September): 18–21.

———. 1991. "Multicultural Mathematics Education for the Middle Grades." *Arithmetic Teacher* 38(February): 8–13.

———. 1993a. *Multicultural Mathematics: Interdisciplinary Cooperative-Learning Activities.* Portland, ME: J. Weston Walch.

———. 1993b. "Multicultural Mathematics: One Road to the Goal of Mathematics for All." In *Reaching All Students with Mathematics*, edited by G. Cuevas and M. Driscoll, 45–55. Reston, VA: NCTM.

———. 1993c. Letter to the editor. *Arithmetic Teacher* 41(October): 114.

———. 1994a. *Fear of Math: How to Get Over It and Get On with Your Life.* New Brunswick, NJ: Rutgers University Press.

———. 1994b. *Multicultural Math: Hands-On Activities from Around the World.* New York: Scholastic Professional.

Index

The author and publisher wish to thank those who have generously given permission to reprint borrowed material:

Excerpts from "Contextualized Mathematics Instruction: Moving Beyond Recent Proposals" by Heckman, P.E., and J. Weissglass. From *For the Learning of Mathematics* (vol. 14, no. 1, February, 1994). Reprinted by permission of Julian Weissglass.

Figures 5–1, 8–7, 9–8 and left-hand figure on page 196: From *Multicultural Mathematics: Interdisciplinary Cooperative Learning Activities* by Claudia Zaslavsky. Copyright © 1993 by J. Weston Walch. Reprinted by permission of the publisher. Further reproduction prohibited.

Figures 6–1 and those on pages 195–197: From *Africa Counts: Number and Pattern in African Culture* by Claudia Zaslavsky. Copyright © 1973 by Claudia Zaslavsky. Reprinted by permission of Lawrence Hill Books.

Figure 9–6: Adapted from *African Designs from Traditional Sources* by Geoffrey Williams. Copyright © 1971. Published by Dover Publications. Used by permission.

"Come to Where the Cancer Is" and "Pack of Lies" by Melissa Antonow and Caheim Drake. From *Kids Don't Smoke*. Reprinted by permission of SmokeFree Educational Services.